THE FIRST
IRISH
RAILWAY

THE FIRST IRISH RAILWAY

WESTLAND ROW TO KINGSTOWN

KURT KULLMANN

The
History
Press

The runaway train went over the hill,
And the last we heard, she was goin' still

First published 2018

The History Press Ireland
50 City Quay
Dublin 2
Ireland
www.thehistorypress.ie

The History Press Ireland is a member of Publishing Ireland,
the Irish book publishers' association.

British Library Cataloguing in Publication Data.
A catalogue record for this book is available from the British Library.

ISBN 978 0 7509 8764 6

Typesetting and origination by The History Press
Printed and bound by TJ International Ltd

Contents

In memoriam
Clemens Alexander Joseph Winterscheid (1843–1927),
Köln-Mindener Eisenbahn
Wilhelm Winterscheid (1871–1948), Kölner Straßenbahnen

Michael Cremen (1838–1922), Great Southern & Western Railway
Patrick Donovan (1841–1881), Cork and Bandon Railway

Acknowledgements and Reminiscences

The greatest thanks go, as always, to my wife Catherine, *née* Donovan. She is great at finding sources and discussing sections of my books. Her memories are invaluable to me, as she grew up on a street that runs parallel to the first Irish railway line.

For my own interest in anything that travels on rails, I have to thank my late parents, Carl Kullmann and Dr Maria Theresia Kullmann, *née* Winterscheid. I was a little more than 6 years old when my older brother and I found an electric railway under the Christmas tree. This electric railway evolved into a rather complex system over the next ten years.

Until my early teen years, I grew up in a West German market garden village, which meant that any shopping other than victuals had to be done in nearby towns, the bigger ones being Bonn and Cologne. Both of these were reached by a private railway (standard gauge).

Once I had started secondary school, this railway was also used to travel to school, until we moved to a town to the east of Cologne. This town had train and tram connections with Cologne. We lived beside the railway line, next to a level crossing. My path to school followed, at least in parts, this railway line. Shopping, going to cinemas or theatres or visiting relations usually meant using the tram, which went much more frequently than the train.

I started my studies at the University of Würzburg, where I encountered a narrow-gauge tram system. I still remember the screeching of the old tram cars when they went around sharp corners. Not that I used the tram much. Würzburg is a compact town and my budget was low, so I usually walked.

Würzburg was around 300km away from home. I went there by train at the beginning of each term and travelled home again by train at the end of each term. During my first years, these trains were still pulled by steam engines. I usually enjoyed the journey home for Christmas, which involved crossing the hills of the Spessart and going along the Rhine when everything was white with snow. However, there was one time when traffic was heavy and I had to take an additional train made up of old carriages. Unluckily, those old carriages had not been checked extensively and we soon discovered that the heating system had broken down. We spent four hours in an icy-cold compartment, huddled in our thick winter coats, watching the condensation freeze on the inside of the window.

My last student 'action' in Würzburg included my longest train journey ever. I was studying mineralogy and the university had organised an excursion to inspect some working mines – in Turkey. First we had to go from Würzburg to Munich, which took a couple of hours. In Munich, we had to change trains. The train journey from Munich to Istanbul took a day and a half. Most of us students did not have the money for a bed in a sleeper. We arranged ourselves as best as we could in our compartment. I, as one of the two youngest and lightest, was elected to sleep in the luggage rack. I remember that I slept surprisingly well that night.

In Bonn, where I continued my studies, the tram situation was the same as in Würzburg, except that I walked beside tram tracks of standard gauge instead of narrow gauge. But I had experiences with trains nonetheless, although not so much as a passenger. One of the main north–south railway lines of Germany was built right through the middle of the city of Bonn. There were lots of level crossings and lots of trains. This led to the saying, 'I studied in Bonn for nine terms, which includes the three terms that I had to wait at a level crossing'.

As a mature student in Cologne, I drove myself to classes and meetings with my tutor. By that time, the tram systems of Cologne and Bonn had been combined. They also had been put underground in places.

At that stage I was married and had a family. I had also become interested in family history. I discovered that my great-grandfather Clemens Alexander Joseph Winterscheid started his working career as brakeman on the Köln-Mindener Eisenbahn and worked his way up to technician and finally railway engineer. At that stage, Germany, like Ireland, had a lot of private railway companies that shared their names with their railway termini. My great-grandfather's eldest son, my grandfather Wilhelm Winterscheid, was also a railway engineer. He did not work with trains, though, but with the trams in Cologne.

When we finally came (back) to Ireland, we moved into Catherine's parents' house with her widowed father. As I mentioned before, this house is on a street that runs parallel to the railway line that was formerly the Dublin & Kingstown Railway. Our part of this street is nearly exactly 100 years younger than the railway line.

I was kept busy with family history – there was a whole new branch to be researched – and so I discovered that Catherine had two great-grandfathers who had been involved in railways: Patrick Donovan was, at least at the end of his short life, an engine driver, most likely on the Cork and Bandon Railway, and Michael Cremen started as stoker and worked his way up to engine driver on the Great Southern & Western Railway. He actually drove the first train from Tralee to Cahersiveen. Later he worked on the Cork–Tralee route.

There have been many changes in railways, even in the nearly seventy years during which I have been interested in anything that travels on rails. This book is one of the results of that interest. I dedicate it to all the people mentioned, but especially to my grandfather, my great-grandfather and my two great-grandfathers-in-law.

A heartfelt thank you is due to John Eugene Mullee of Houston, Texas, who grew up around the corner from the house my wife Catherine grew up in, so that he could look into our back garden from the back bedrooms in his house. He, like me, for some years used the train to go to school as well and his memories were very helpful, especially as he used the stretch from Sandymount to Westland Row.

Special thanks go to Ciarán Cooney of the IRRS and Charles Friel of the RPSI, who provided photographs and information. Thank you also to those who allowed me to reproduce photographs: Albert Bridge, Keith Edkins, Harold Falye, Michael Costello.

Abbreviations

AIB	Allied Irish Bank
CC	Cricket Club
CDJR	City of Dublin Junction Railway (known as the Loop Line)
CIÉ	Córas Iompair Éireann
DART	Dublin Area Rapid Transit
D&KR	Dublin and Kingstown Railway
DSE	Dublin and South Eastern Railway (also known locally as Dublin Slow and Easy)
D&SER	Dublin and South Eastern Railway
DUTC	Dublin United Tram Company (1891–1941)
DUTC	Dublin United Transport Company (1941–1945)
DW&WR	Dublin, Wicklow and Wexford Railway
ESB	Electricity Supply Board
FC	Football Club
GSR	Great Southern Railway
GS&WR	Great Southern and Western Railway
IÉ	Iarnród Éireann
IRRS	Irish Railway Record Society
IT	Information Technology
L&MR	Liverpool and Manchester Railway
NIR	Northern Ireland Railway
OS	Ordnance Survey
RDS	Royal Dublin Society
RPSI	Railway Preservation Society of Ireland
S&DR	Stockton and Darlington Railway
SDUK	Society for the Diffusion of Useful Knowledge
TCD	Trinity College Dublin
UIC	Union Internationale des Chemins de Fer (International Union of Railways)
WWW&DR	Waterford, Wexford, Wicklow and Dublin Railway

Preliminary Remarks

Transport on rails or fixed routes of one type or other is a very old form of transport. Possibly the best-known example from antiquity is the Diolkos on the Isthmus of Corinth, on which ships were pulled 6.4km (4 miles) over the isthmus between the Saronic Gulf and the Gulf of Corinth, saving them the long and dangerous circumnavigation of the Peloponnese. It was used from around 600 BCE (Before Common Era) to around 50 CE. (Common Era).

In the late Middle Ages, miners used carts to transport the ore out of their tunnels in the mountains. Those carts had wheels that sometimes ran

Miner with mine car running in grooves.

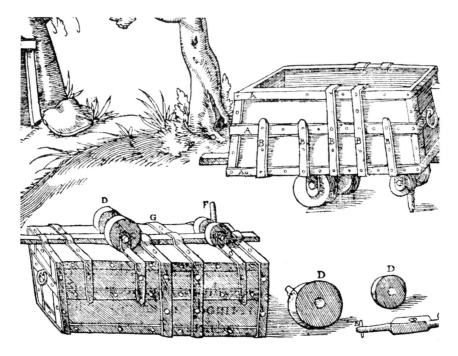

Mining car; F denotes the pin that runs in a central groove.

in grooves or that had a pin that ran in a central groove to keep the laden carts running the way they were expected to run, especially in the dark environment of an underground mine.

The woodcut on the preceding page shows the grooves in which the wheels of the little car roll. The above woodcut, from the same book, shows another system with a pin underneath the car that runs in a central groove.

What we regard as a railway now is quite different. Again, rails for transporting goods and passengers were known for quite some time before the first railways, as we know them, were built. Their precursors were pushed by people or pulled by horses, whereas our idea of a railway is based on trains being pulled by some kind of engine. The railway era, in this sense, started with steam engines.

In the Beginning was the Steam

Steam engine, machine using steam power to perform mechanical work through the agency of heat.[1]

The first known device that used steam to set something in motion was the Aeolipile, a steam turbine invented in the first century CE by Heron of Alexandria. The first commercially used steam engine with a piston was the atmospheric engine of Thomas Newcomen (1664–1729). Newcomen constructed this in 1712 to pump water out of a mine. In general, the person most thought of when talking about early steam engines is the Scottish inventor James Watt (1736–1819), who improved Newcomen's engine in such a way that it could be used for all sorts of different work in different situations.

Those steam engines were stationary. During the first quarter of the nineteenth century, inventors experimented with steam engines on wheels. The *Encyclopaedia Britannica* defines a railway as follows:

A railroad (or railway) is a mode of land transportation in which freight-goods and passenger-carrying vehicles, or cars, with flanged wheels move over two parallel steel rails.[2]

This definition does not say anything about the power that is used for this land transportation. In general, it is locomotives, moveable engines, powered by steam in the beginning, that come to mind when thinking or talking about a railway:

13

A steam engine is by nature a small explosion of power. It claims most of your senses – not just your eyes and ears – especially if you are standing on the edge of the railway platform as it thunders past without stopping. Even standing close to a steam engine when it is only starting to move is an exhilarating experience.[3]

Plans for the First Irish Railway

The first public railway line with steam locomotives was the Stockton and Darlington Railway (S&DR) which opened on 27 September 1825. During its first years, it only transported goods (mainly coal) in trains pulled by steam engines; passenger carriages were still pulled by horses. The first public railway using steam engines to transport passengers was the Liverpool and Manchester Railway (L&MR), which opened on 15 September 1830. This was the beginning of the development of railways, which ultimately became so frenzied that it was called 'railway mania'. Railways were regarded as a good investment and every area wanted at least one railway line. Railways were run by publicly subscribed private companies that usually had the termini in their names (S&DR, L&MR, D&KR) until some of those companies merged and the companies' names described the area they worked in (D&SER, GS&WR, GSR). Ireland got its first railway in 1834.

Also in the Beginning was: The Royal Mail

Even after the union of Ireland with Great Britain on 1 January 1801, the mail service between London and Dublin was very important, despite the fact that Dublin had lost its function as a capital. Originally mail boats travelled to Poolbeg, near Ringsend. When ships became bigger, this stopping place a few miles east of Dublin, which had never been quite satisfactory, became too difficult to reach. Sailing up to Dublin on the Liffey was no longer an option as the water was not deep enough, but even anchoring places like Poolbeg were not easy to reach due to the many, often shifting, sandbanks across the mouth of the Liffey, where it flows into Dublin Bay:

> Many ships were grounded as there was only a narrow path through the sandbanks to the river mouth. It needed skilled captains to negotiate the dangers. Because of this, there was a huge waiting time. Ships were anchored out there for days before being allowed in.[4]

But more and more freight had to be shifted into and out of the growing city, with bulky goods like coal coming from across the Irish Sea.

At the beginning of the nineteenth century, Ringsend/Poolbeg/ Pigeonhouse was definitely no longer an adequate port for Dublin. Despite the fact that Dublin was not a capital city any more, good mail connections were still very important. Waiting times on the Irish side needed to be eliminated as quickly as possible.

A new harbour was planned. Howth, which already had a fishing harbour, was chosen. Unfortunately, the position for Howth Harbour was decided upon without listening to the local experts and the newly built harbour began to silt up almost immediately. The mail boat service had been given to Howth in 1818, but not much more than fifteen years later, the harbour had been filled with so much silt and sand that it was much less deep than it had been originally and the mail boats had become longer and wider and, significantly, had a bigger loaded draught. Thus, it was no longer practicable to send the mail boats to Howth. On the other side of the Irish Sea, the Menai Bridge had been built in 1826 to eliminate the necessity of crossing the Menai Strait by ship, thus shortening the time the Royal Mail needed to reach Dublin from Holyhead. With those bigger mail boats and the pressure to shorten the time of the journey between London and Dublin, Howth Harbour was no longer adequate.

What is now known as Dún Laoghaire Harbour was originally planned as an asylum harbour for ships in distress. The first stone was officially laid in May 1817. Soon, this harbour was given other functions, even before it was finished in 1842. The first steamboats coming from Liverpool were too big for Howth and travelled to Kingstown (Dún Laoghaire) from 1826. The official Royal Mail went from Holyhead and used Howth until April 1834, when the harbour of Kingstown was finally chosen for the Royal Mail. From there, it was brought to Dublin by government coaches during the period from April 1834 to April 1835, whereupon the railway took over. In 1848, the railway link between London and Holyhead was completed, which improved the speed of the service enormously.

Yet Another Beginning:
The Asylum Harbour

Frequent and violent eastern gales led to many shipwrecks in Dublin Bay up until the eighteenth century, as there was no safe place for ships seeking protection from inclement weather. The double catastrophe of the *Rochdale* and the *Prince of Wales* in 1807, with the loss of hundreds of lives, was the last straw. The cry for an asylum harbour could not be ignored any more. An asylum harbour, however, could only be built at a location where the sea was sufficiently deep until quite near the land, which ruled out anywhere around the mouth of the Liffey. The small fishing village of Dunleary was chosen as the location for this new harbour. Dunleary had a tiny pier already, but this was not at all sufficient for what was intended. And so it was that between 1817 and 1842, the biggest man-made harbour of Western Europe was built 15km (9.3 miles) south-east of Dublin's city centre.

What became the port of Kingstown (later Dún Laoghaire) was originally planned as an asylum harbour, a place where ships in distress could find shelter from the frequent, strong easterly gales on the Irish Sea. Soon it became much more.

King George IV left Ireland from this harbour at the end of his visit in 1821, which gave a big boost to the community that had started to grow on the hill above the harbour and which had been quite small until then. To commemorate the king's visit, they chose to rename the village, which soon grew into a small town, 'Kingstown'. The increasing number of ships at the new harbour led to different surveys and plans for getting the goods to Dublin. This became a more pressing concern when Kingstown took over from Howth as the Irish port for all mail boats. The original asylum harbour for ships in distress had definitely developed into a 'normal' harbour for goods and passengers and, of course, for the Royal Mail.

The first idea for getting the goods to Dublin City had been to transport them by boat on a canal that would connect the KingstownHarbour with the Grand Canal Basin between Dublin City and Ringsend. Not much later, others proposed connecting the city with the port using a railway line. It took some time before the proponents of the railway won over the group favouring a canal. The increasing number of passengers that arrived in this harbour might have influenced the decision. And so Ireland got her first railway, a couple of years later than England and France, but a year earlier than Germany.

The comings and goings of ships had made Kingstown interesting and soon rich citizens from Dublin built villas and residences there, e.g. Thomas M. Gresham, the owner of Gresham's Hotel on Sackville Street (now O'Connell Street). Investors were of the opinion that a railway line from Dublin to its new developing harbour and the growing communities of well-to-do people on the southern side of Dublin Bay might be a good idea. Gresham and others objected for different reasons at first, but finally they withdrew their objections, for a price, of course. According to earlier plans for the harbour, the railway was originally only intended to reach the place where the Salthill and Monkstown stop is now, as the pier for the mail boats was planned for that location, near the western pier of the new harbour. When the plans for the harbour changed, the railway plans had to be changed as well and the line was going to be extended to where Dún Laoghaire Station is now. After Carlisle Pier had been built in 1859, a further extension was planned, bringing the railway to this pier to meet the boats.

Some Worries

There were different types of worries: worries about getting parliament to agree to the railway company's building of the rail line, worries about raising the money and choosing the best possible route. But there were other worries, some possibly justified, but many not, worries like those of Mr Gresham and other citizens of Kingstown, who, on the one hand, did not want the plebs overrunning their nice, middle-class residential area for well-to-do citizens, but, on the other hand, wanted to get other middle-class citizens from Dublin to spend their money in Kingstown and not to go on to Bray. Some of those worries would, in modern parlance, be labelled NIMBY (Not In My Back-Yard). Others had worries that would nowadays be regarded as the BANANA attitude (Build Absolutely Nothing Anywhere Near Anything), which is the general attitude of people who do not want development: no new inventions, no new roads (rail or otherwise), no new neighbours, no new ideas. The words/acronyms might be new, but the attitudes are ancient and so, naturally, were in evidence at the time of the proposal to build a railway.

Some people were of the opinion that subjecting a human being to a speed of more than 25mph (40km/h) would have a lasting negative effect on the human brain and lead to insanity. Some other worries were dealt with in an article in volume 63 of *The Quarterly Review*, which tried to reassure potential passengers that not only were railroads safer than roads, as there was no traffic and the line was smooth, without sharp bends or hard climbs, but also that railway carriages were safer than a stage coach as their centre of gravity was lower and consequently they would not topple over. Unlike horses, locomotives would not run away, tumble down or shy away from strange objects. As far as the danger of momentum was concerned, they used the wisdom of old soldiers 'calming' new recruits who were afraid of artillery by telling them that 'a musket ball kills a man as dead as a cannon-shot'.[5] Concerning fatalities, the article states that between 1831 and 1838 only around a dozen of over 44 million railway passengers had been killed.[6]

For the shareholders of the Dublin & Kingstown Railway Company, it should have been reassuring that of those 44 million passengers, more than half (26,410,152) were passengers of the D&KR in the short time between mid-November 1836 and the end of August 1838. There were five fatalities on the D&KR during this time; some of these were possibly due to the fact that, at that time, the sides of third-class carriages only came up to waist height and had no doors at all – there were just open gaps where passengers could get in and out. It has to be remembered, of course, that people in third class (or indeed any other class) had no idea of the effect of falling from a speeding train that might go as fast as 40mph (65km/h) or even faster. Jumping on and off a moving bus was still quite common in the second half of the twentieth century after all, and lasted as long as buses had open platforms.

The owners of hackney cars naturally had their own concerns and saw the railway as very strong competition. Their concerns were obviously unfounded:

> The Dublin and Kingstown railway has been in operation for three years only. The prices are not lower than those of the ordinary road conveyances; and the line being a very short one, no considerable saving is effected in point of time; yet it has more traffic than ever was known to be on the high road, while the latter is still frequented to a great extent, with carriages, horses, and foot passengers. The owners of hackney cars, who had derived all their support from the intercourse between Dublin and Kingstown, and feared that they would be thrown out of bread by the railway, have actually experienced an improvement of their business – not all, indeed, being employed upon the same line as before – but finding the deficit amply made up by calls to places not directly in the line of the railway, and in journeys and excursions to and from its several stations.[7]

The company had its own worries concerning passengers. There was enough checking of tickets that it would not have been easy to use the train without a valid ticket, but it often happened that passengers with second-class tickets used first-class carriages. Another problem, which was an even bigger issue in terms of its implications for the safety of passengers, was that that some passengers, obviously from the old custom with mail and stage coaches, travelled on the roofs of the carriages, despite the fact that the train travelled considerably faster than a coach. This practice was finally strictly forbidden when the first extension (from Salthill to Kingstown) was finished, as this included a bridge that had so little headroom for the carriages that there was no room for passengers on the roofs of the carriages.

Later, other worries surfaced, some caused by technical problems, e.g. it had not been foreseen that granite sleepers were bad for the tracks and so they had to be replaced by wooden sleepers, platforms had to be built, as well as footbridges, using a material that would not get slippery when wet.

At least the D&KR, in general, made a good profit, so that the company could pay decent dividends to their shareholders. Not all railway companies were so lucky.

Companies and Lines

The Dublin and Kingstown Railway Company was founded in 1831. The railway line was opened in 1834. Even before that, the company had been thinking of extending the line. In 1843, the D&KR built the Atmospheric Railway from Kingstown to Dalkey. In 1854, the whole line from Westland Row to Dalkey was leased to the Waterford, Wexford, Wicklow and Dublin Railway Company (WWW&DR), which then changed the gauge on the whole stretch from Westland Row to Dalkey from what is today known as the standard gauge or international gauge (1,435mm/4ft 8½in) to the Irish gauge (1,600mm/5ft 3in), which is still in use all over Ireland. In 1860, the WWW&DR changed its name to Dublin, Wicklow and Wexford Railway (DW&WR). In the 1860s, the line was extended to Enniscorthy and in the 1870s it finally reached Wexford. This railway company changed its name again in 1906 to Dublin and South Eastern Railway, with the abbreviation D&SER or simply DSE. The fact that this last abbreviation was said to stand for 'Dublin Slow and Easy' for years shows the affection and/or the annoyance that it evoked in its customers.

After rapidly expanding at first, with a peak in 1920, when Ireland had 5,600km (3,480 miles) of railway, the network began to shrink. In the second decade of the twenty-first century, the railway network of Ireland (all thirty-two counties) is around 2,700km (1,675 miles), 53km (33 miles) of which is electrified and around 360km (225 miles) is only for freight trains.

In 1925, all railway companies in Saorstát Éireann were combined to form the Great Southern Railway (GSR), which in 1945 amalgamated with the Dublin United Transport Company (DUTC) to form Córas Iompair Éireann (CIÉ). Since 1986, CIÉ has acted as the holding company for the companies Iarnród Éireann/Irish Rail, Bus Éireann and Dublin Bus. Iarnród Éireann (IÉ) runs all those rail lines still in existence in the Republic, including the Dublin Area Rapid Transit (DART), whereas the six counties of the north-east are served by Northern Ireland Railways (NIR). The route from Dublin to Belfast is served jointly by IÉ and NIR.

The stretch that used to be the Dublin & Kingstown Railway has been electrified since the early 1980s, and is now used by the electric trains of the DART and the diesel-electric multiple units of the commuter line to Drogheda and Dundalk in the north, and to Bray, Greystones and Gorey in the south, as well as the intercity trains to Wexford and Rosslare Harbour. Until the end of 2002, there were regular goods trains from Dublin to the fertilizer factory in Arklow. Since the closing of this factory in October 2002, there have been no more regular freight trains on that stretch of the former D&KR.

This book is only concerned with the railway stretch between Dublin Pearse Station (formerly Westland Row Station) and Dún Laoghaire Mallin Station (formerly Kingstown Station), a very short stretch on the longest connected Irish railway route, which stretches from Derry in the north-west via Belfast and Dublin to Rosslare Harbour in the south-east, even though there are no trains that travel the whole route.

On the short stretch that is described in these pages, there are eighty-five passenger trains travelling in each direction every workday between 6.30 a.m. and 11.30 p.m., not counting the shifting of empty trains or occasional service trains. This makes it one of the most used stretches of railway in Ireland, as well as the one most cursed by car drivers. The Loop Line from Pearse to Connolly has an even higher frequency of trains, but it has neither stops nor level crossings and so is spared the motorists' curses.

The Route

Problems with the termini at either end of the line were by no means the only difficulties the company that was going to build the Dublin and Kingstown Railway (D&KR) had to deal with. There were problems with parliament, which had to approve the route. There were problems with landowners like Baron Cloncurry of Maretimo and the Rev. Sir Harcourt Lees of Blackrock House, both in Blackrock, who strongly objected that the railway line was cutting their residences off from their access to the sea. Rather large sums of money were paid out as compensation for the inconveniences caused to those landowners and in both cases private bridges were built across the railway line, though the one for Lord Cloncurry was and remains much grander than the one built for the Rev. Sir Harcourt Lees. Further details about the parliamentary process and discussions with landowners and residents are described by K. A. Murray.[8]

The map shows that the railway runs along the shortest feasible line between the two termini. This caused a few more problems, as some stretches actually went through the sea and one stretch had to be cut through a rocky promontory. The difficulties started with the termini – or rather with their

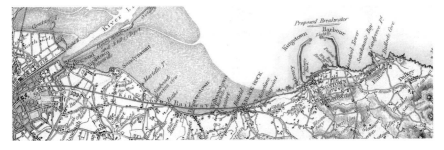

Map of the route of the Dublin & Kingstown Railway. Drawn and engraved by B.R. Davies for the Society for the Diffusion of Useful Knowledge (SDUK), 1837.

exact location. The Dublin terminus was originally planned for a place at the western end of Great Brunswick Street (now Pearse Street), near the southern end of Hawkins Street. Understandably, both Dublin University and the residents of Great Brunswick Street objected to having a railway line between the end of their back gardens and the university grounds. This meant that the line could only start at Westland Row. At the other end, the line originally terminated where the Salthill and Monkstown stop is now, as the original plan of the harbour commissioners had been to build a wharf for the mail boats near the tiny old harbour of the small fishing village of Dunleary. But the harbour commissioners changed their plans and built the wharf for the mail boats much nearer the east pier. Subsequently the railway was extended to the place where Dún Laoghaire Mallin Station is now.

Within the built-up area of Dublin City, i.e. from Westland Row to Grand Canal Dock, the railway line crosses five streets: South Cumberland Street, Sandwith Street, Erne Street, Great Clarence Street (now Macken Street) and Grand Canal Quay. Grand Canal Dock also had to be crossed. As Grand Canal Dock definitely demanded a bridge, it was decided that the railway should be elevated at least until Grand Canal Dock, so that the five streets between the Grand Canal and Westland Row were crossed on bridges as well. That way, traffic on those streets would not be disturbed by frequent trains.

The railway did not cross those bridges at a right angle. The angles between the railway and the road differed quite a lot. Cumberland Street South had the least skew angle (i.e. the angle of deviation from a right angle) of only 4 degrees.[9]

From Grand Canal Dock, the railway line gradually approached ground level, but the first three streets after Grand Canal Dock – Barrow Street, South Lotts Road and Bath Avenue – still had to be crossed on bridges. Some of these bridges were very low and later led to difficulties when trams ran on Bath Avenue, especially as the Bath Avenue bridge, apart from its low headroom, has a skew angle of 33°45', which made this low thoroughfare longer than any of the others.

The Dodder also had to be crossed, so another bridge was necessary, but this could be rather low as there had never been any shipping on the Dodder. From Haig's Lane (now Lansdowne Road), the railway line crossed roads at ground level, which led to the level crossings on Lansdowne Road, Serpentine Avenue, Sandymount Lane (now Sandymount Avenue), Sydney Parade and Strand Road (Merrion Gates), all of which are still there, the only level crossings on the entire D&KR line. At the time the railway was built, this was not such a big problem as the area was not as densely populated as it is nowadays. By now, not only has the population of the area grown considerably, but motorisation has increased, as for any household without a car, there is at least one with two or even more cars. Thus, those level crossings are often cursed by car drivers and not only by those in a hurry.

It is well known that the line was built by the Irishman William Dargan (1799–1867). The engineer who planned the building of the line, however, was the Irish-born Charles Blacker Vignoles. It is interesting to note that on his 1834 map of the railway line and its surroundings, a street bridge across the Dodder is shown at Haig's Distillery, whereas the 1843 OS map only shows the possibility of crossing the river on a weir at that point.

From Merrion Gates, other problems arose. The shortest line from there to Blackrock actually led across the water and that is exactly where Vignoles had the line built. The route crosses the water from Merrion Gates, touching land at the Williamstown Martello tower before crossing the water again to Blackrock and touching land at the spot where the station is now, after which it cuts off a few more parts of the sea at Seapoint and Monkstown. The smaller parts were quickly filled in and a bigger lagoon was turned into Blackrock Park after it had been filled, but the stretch between Merrion Gates and Williamstown remained a lagoon with, at times, very disagreeable effects due to the water getting stagnant and emitting foul odours. The Booterstown stop, then as now, could only be reached by a causeway across the lagoon.

Before the railway line was finally opened for the public on 17 December 1834, there were a couple of trial runs and then a ceremonial run for invited dignitaries only. A story reports that a young man of around 20 considered this a challenge, as he was one of a group of lads that prided themselves on being able to manage being part of anything that was invitation–only, even if they had not been invited. He took bets that he would be on that train without an invitation. He used the footbridge at the Westland Row terminus, which was meant for crossing from one platform to the other, positioned himself directly over the train, waiting just under this footbridge, and when the train started to move, he dropped onto the roof of one of the carriages. He held on tight and actually managed to stay safe as far as the Salthill terminus. When he was discovered, some of the invited travellers congratulated him on his feat, but nobody shook hands with him. The young man had not reckoned with the soot. He had to throw his clothes away and it was said that it took him weeks to get the soot out of his hair and skin. He probably spent quite a few days coughing as well.

Originally, the line was supposed to be opened in summer 1834, but unforeseen difficulties both with the elevated stretch and the stretch through the sea caused the opening to be postponed. Finally, a time in November was chosen, but even that deadline could not be met. This time, it was the fault of the River Dodder. The Dublin Annals at the end of an almanac record:

> 1834 Inundation of the Dodder, whereby a temporary bridge at Ball's-bridge was carried away, the neighbouring country flooded, and much injury done to the buildings of the Railway. Dec. 17th, Railway between Dublin and Kingstown opened for the public.[10]

During the first years of the railway line, there were some poor cottagers living in the area the line crossed, but as the region between Dublin and Kingstown (Dún Laoghaire) was a favourite place for well-to-do Dublin citizens to build residences outside the city, the line seems to have done quite well, as William Makepeace Thackeray mentions in 1842:

> It is the continual appearance of this sort of wealth which makes the poverty more striking: and thus between the two (for there is no vacant space of fields between Kingstown and Dublin) the car reaches the city. There is but little commerce on the road, which was also in extremely bad repair. It is neglected for the sake of its thriving neighbour the railroad; on which a dozen pretty little stations accommodate the inhabitants of the various villages through which we pass.[11]

Of course, Thackeray did not know that the Rock Road was in an appalling state even before the railway came and as the authority that was responsible for the road, the Grand Jury, had nothing to do with the railway company, the observation that the road was neglected in favour of the railway was unfounded. His remark about 'a dozen little stations' is an exaggeration as well. It was in 1842 that Thackeray was driven in a cab from Kingstown to Dublin; the 1843 OS map shows only four stations between Kingstown and Westland Row – Salthill and Monkstown, Blackrock, Williamstown and Booterstown – though some descriptions of the line mention stations at Sandymount and Merrion at that time as well.

As far as costs are concerned, the building of the Dublin & Kingstown Railway seems to have been much more expensive than the building of other lines. An 1839 article quoting the Royal Commission gives the following amounts in pounds per mile:

American railways	from £6,000
Future Irish railways	£10,000
French railways	£15,000
Liverpool and Manchester Railway	£30,000
Dublin & Kingstown Railway	£40,000[12]

The high price per mile for the Dublin & Kingstown Railway might have had something to do with the fact that the line included eight bridges over streets, apart from the bridges crossing the Grand Canal Basin and the Dodder. Also, building the line involved building a causeway across a part of the sea, cutting through rock between Blackrock and Seapoint and the structures to be erected for Lord Cloncurry and the Rev. Sir Harcourt Lees, plus the payments to those two gentlemen for being allowed to build the line across their properties. Those payments (without the costs for the additional structures) amounted to £10,500. As the line was originally less than 6 miles long, these costs must have increased the price per mile considerably.

Engineers, Builders and Architects

Charles Blacker Vignoles (1793–1875) is usually described as an eminent British railway engineer, but he was born in Woodbrook, Co. Wexford. His father was in the army and during the wars with France was sent to the West Indies with his wife and his infant son. A battle was lost and the family was captured by the French. Both father and mother died of yellow fever and Charles, little more than 1 year old then, was cared for by his uncle, who finally managed to get him back to the UK. Charles studied mathematics and law, but then started an army career. After the end of the Napoleonic Wars, he worked as an engineer in America and England, where he became interested in railways. He went to Ireland and planned the first Irish railway, the Dublin & Kingstown Railway. For the D&KR, he designed the Westland Row terminus building. He planned and designed the whole line and did work for the D&KR from 1832 to 1834. From 1836 to 1838, he was engineer to the royal commission on railways in Ireland. In the 1840s, he worked for the D&KR again, as the engineer for the Atmospheric Railway between Kingstown (Dún Laoghaire) and Dalkey. He also worked on tunnels, bridges and canals in various countries.

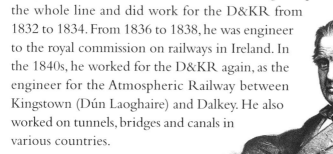

Charles Blacker Vignoles.

William Dargan.

He later worked in the Ukraine (then part of the Russian Empire), the German Herzogtum Nassau and again in England, as well as in Spain and Brazil, mainly for railway companies. He retired in 1863. In 1836, he recommended the use of rails in the shape they still have now: so-called flat-bottomed rails or flanged T rails, which are today often referred to as Vignoles rails in his honour. Vignoles rails were widely used on the Continent from the earliest times in railway history, but only became widely used in Britain and Ireland during the twentieth century.

William Dargan (1799–1867) was born near Carlow town and is regarded as 'the father of Irish railways'. He is thought to have been the most important Irish engineer of the nineteenth century. In 1833, he got the contract to build the first Irish railway between Dublin and Kingstown (now Dún Laoghaire). Altogether, Dargan built over 1,300km (800 miles) of railway in Ireland and made a fortune. He was also influential in the establishment of the National Gallery of Ireland, which is why his statue stands in front of this gallery to this day. He was responsible, too, for the Great Dublin Exhibition in 1853.

John Skipton Mulvany.

Sir Thomas Newenham Deane.

During this exhibition, Dargan was honoured by a visit by Queen Victoria at his private residence. As he was very patriotic, he declined the queen's offer of a baronetcy. As an indication of the size of his fortune, it should be mentioned that for the Great Dublin Exhibition in 1853, he advanced £100,000 altogether. Financially, the exhibition was not a success and Dargan personally carried a loss of £20,000 (around 2.5 million Euro today). Later in life, he was chairman of the DW&WR and worked on its extension, though he did not live to see its completion to Wexford. He died in Dublin in 1867 after a fall from his horse. In the twenty-first century, the new cable-stayed Luas bridge in Dundrum was named the William Dargan Bridge in his honour.

John Skipton Mulvany (1813–1870) was born either in Sandymount or in Blackrock. He was the fourth son of the painter and first keeper of the Royal Hibernian Academy Thomas James Mulvany, whose second son George F. Mulvany became the first director of the National Gallery of Ireland. John Skipton was trained by the architect William Deane Butler, who was the architect of Amiens Street Station (now Connolly Station). He became known while still quite young and worked on the stations of different railway companies. For the Dublin & Kingstown Railway Company, he built the stations in Blackrock, Kingstown (Dún Laoghaire) and the first terminal station in Salthill, which no longer exists. Near the Kingstown terminus of the D&KR, he built, in the same style, both the Royal St George Yacht Club and, a couple of years later, the Royal Irish Yacht Club.

He also produced plans for additions to the Salthill Hotel that was owned by the railway company, as well as building Mount Anville, the residence of the railway engineer William Dargan. For himself, he reserved one of the houses on Brighton Vale that he had designed between the railway and the sea (probably no. 5).

Sir Thomas Newenham Deane (1828–1899) was trained by his father Sir Thomas Deane and became a partner in his father's business, together with Benjamin Woodward. Their firm worked in the Gothic style and built the Museum Building in Trinity College Dublin, the Kildare Street Club and the National Museum and National Library on Kildare Street.

He was involved in the rebuilding of the Westland Row Terminal of the then D&SER in 1884. The façade he designed for it had to be changed when the Loop Line (officially the CDJR) was built in 1891.

Termini

The original plan of having the Dublin terminus of the line at the western end of Trinity College could not be carried out, but the location of the terminus that was finally chosen (and is still in use today, though it is no longer a terminus) is beside some buildings at the eastern end of Trinity College, with further college buildings north and west of it. The original building originated from a design by Charles Vignoles.

As the railway line was elevated in Dublin, trains arrived on the first floor of the terminus building. The ground floor had offices and, as is evidenced by the door for carriages on the right, the loading/unloading station for the Royal Mail. An early guide describes the building thus:

> The front of the entrance is plain, but the interior of the building is very convenient; the waiting-rooms for passengers are neatly furnished. The carriages are entered from a yard, a great part of which is covered with an iron roof.[13]

Elevation of station fronting Westland Row.

Kingstown (Dún Laoghaire) Station and Victoria fountain; from an old postcard.

This façade was changed when the station was updated in 1884, with Sir Thomas Newenham Deane as architect. Today, Deane's façade cannot be seen exactly as he designed it because the building of the Loop Line (or the City of Dublin Junction Railway, to give it its full original name) in 1891 necessitated the creation of a huge big opening in the front wall of the station, as seen on Plate 1.

The contractor for those alterations was Michael Meade & Sons of Ballsbridge, which was, at that time, part of Pembroke Township (now Dublin 4). The curved roof of the train hall was built based on plans by Richard Turner, the owner of the Hammersmith Ironworks, also in Ballsbridge. The main roof is 155m (510ft) long and spans nearly 27m (90ft); the smaller bay to the south-west is 73m (240ft) long and has a span of almost 20m (65ft).[14]

Nothing is left of the original southern terminus, the one at the old Dunleary Harbour, near where the west pier is now. The original building was designed by John Skipton Mulvany, but when the line reached that point, the extension for a further half mile had already been decided upon and the original terminus building at Salthill was taken down. The building usually referred to as the Kingstown terminus of the D&KR is still there. It served as the terminus from 1842 until 1856, the year in which the extension to Dalkey and Bray was opened. The building has remained in service, but no longer as a terminus. Some old postcards seem to be the earliest depictions of it.

Kingstown (Dún Laoghaire) Station showing the train hall; from an old postcard.

Kingstown railway terminus, *c.*1930.

These old postcards do not show any sign of an extension, but that does not mean that they depict the situation as it was before the extension was built. From the time of the Atmospheric Railway, which started in 1844, the last, westernmost stretch of the Atmospheric Railway, before it reached its terminus at Kingstown (Dún Laoghaire), was in a tunnel. It is likely that the first postcard shows the view from around 1875. Both this postcard and the postcard below it show the building that was probably the station building of the Atmospheric Railway, as it is facing the last stretch of the rail of that line.

The old postcards show the train hall from the time when Kingstown (Dún Laoghaire) was the terminus of the line. It seems likely that this hall was not there from the beginning, as the 1843 OS map does not show a building with a roof over the tracks. After it had been erected, this hall held two tracks under its roof. The roof is still shown on the 1912 OS map. Today it has disappeared, although the walls of the hall and one of the two tracks also are still there.

Seen from Queen's Road, as in the photograph from the 1930s, it looks as if the building only has one storey. The rails and platforms are one storey lower as the extended line through Dalkey and Bray starts under the surface of Queen's Road.

Today it does not look much different (see Plate 2), except that there is usually more traffic in front of it. In 1966, it was renamed Dún Laoghaire Mallin Station in honour of Michael Thomas Mallin, second in command of the Irish Citizen Army under James Connolly during the Easter Rising of 1916. He commanded the garrison at St Stephen's Green in Dublin, with Constance Markievicz as his second in command. A bronze plaque beside the steps to the entrance bears the inscription:

I GCUIMHNE AR ÉIRÍ AMACH 1916 TUGADH STÁISIÚN Í MHEALLÁIN AR AN

BHFOIRGNEAMH SEO IN ONÓIR DO MHÍCHEÁL Ó MEALLÁIN

TO COMMEMORATE THE 1916 RISING THIS BUILDING WAS NAMED

MALLIN STATION IN HONOUR OF MICHAEL MALLIN

The building was turned into a restaurant in the early 1970s and is still a restaurant in 2017, though under different management and with a different name. The impressive entrance, however, has remained the same.

The architect of this station building was John Skipton Mulvany (1813–1870), who designed a number of train stations: on the D&KR line, for instance, as well as the now demolished Monkstown and Salthill Station (designed in 1837) and the extant Blackrock Station (in 1841) and, after the extension of the line, the Dalkey Railway station. In other words, J.S. Mulvany built all the original stations, with the exception of Westland Row, which was designed by Charles Vignoles, the engineer responsible for

Entrance to the former Dún Laoghaire Railway Station, 2011.

planning the line. Mulvany also built the Broadstone Station in Dublin, as well as railway stations in Mullingar, Athlone and Galway, among others. He was also asked to design additions to the Salthill Hotel for the DK&R Company. Near the station in Dún Laoghaire, he built the Royal St George Yacht Club (1842–3) and the Royal Irish Yacht Club (1847–50).

Stops and Tariffs

Considering that the railway was originally planned with the intention that it would take freight as well as the Royal Mail from Kingstown (Dún Laoghaire) to Dublin, it was understandable that on this line, which was only 10km (6 miles) long, the original plan only provided for one intermediate stop. This was to be in Blackrock. Obviously that stop was important enough for the abovementioned, well-known railway station architect John Skipton Mulvany to design the station building there in 1841. Soon, however, the company discovered that passengers provided a much higher income than any transport of freight or goods:

> From the opening of the railway, on the 17th December, 1834, to the 1st of March, 1836 – a period of one year and seventy-three days – there were 31,890 single journeys by trains, each trip 5⅔ miles. The total number of passengers conveyed was 1,237,000.[15]

These passengers came not only from Dublin, Kingstown (Dún Laoghaire) and Blackrock, but also from several other places in between. In addition to that, sea-bathing was still *en vogue* and as the line ran along the sea, it was decided that it would be profitable to build baths along the tracks which people from Dublin could frequent, using the new railway line. This meant that new stops would have to be established, of course. A number of stops were opened, some of which did not survive long; others were opened, closed and re-opened, in some cases more than once.

During the years between the beginning of the railway in 1834 and 1960, the D&KR and the subsequent railway companies installed a total of ten stops between Westland Row (Pearse Station) and Kingstown/Dún Laoghaire (Mallin Station) on that line. Blackrock was the only stop when the railway line was opened in 1834, but the following year (1835) six more stations were opened or at least planned. One of them, on Serpentine Avenue, was only in service for two months. Again, two years later (1837), when the line finally reached the Kingstown terminus built by John Skipton Mulvany, the line got two more intermediate stops, one at Seapoint and the second, which had been the first terminus, in Salthill. The latter was important for the Salthill Hotel nearby, which was owned by the railway company. (This hotel, which was renovated and extended by John Skipton Mulvany, burnt down in 1970 and was demolished in 1972. The site is now occupied by apartment blocks.) The stop at Lansdowne Road has only existed since 1870. Blackrock and Lansdowne Road stations, as soon as the latter was established, have stayed open until today. Booterstown, Seapoint and Salthill & Monkstown stations were closed in 1960. Sandymount, Sydney Parade and Williamstown were closed in 1841 and Williamstown was never re-opened. Sydney Parade was re-opened in 1862 and stayed open until 1960; Sandymount was open during the years from 1860 to 1862, 1882 to 1901 and 1928 to 1960. Merrion was open until 1862 and then again from 1882 to 1901 and from 1928 to 1929. Between 1960 and 1984, many suburban stations were closed, but the majority re-opened with the establishment of the Dublin Area Rapid Transit (DART). Merrion and Williamstown stations and the short-lived Serpentine Avenue Station were not used again. A new station was opened on 23 January 2001: Grand Canal Dock Station, which serves the many offices in the Grand Canal Dock area, which is home to so many IT firms that it has been given the nickname 'Silicon Docks'.

In the beginning, it was easy to create a stop, as stops consisted only of a strip of gravel alongside the line in each direction. Passengers used the two steps on the carriages to climb up or down and they had to step carefully across the lines, when, for example, they came from Kingstown (Dún Laoghaire) to bathe in the sea in Merrion, Blackrock or Seapoint or when coming from Dublin to go to the village for which the stop was installed. Accidents were inevitable and soon platforms were built, but still the lines had to be crossed without safety measures. Footbridges were suggested by the railway engineer in 1843, but they only began to be built from 1878 on. There had been wooden footbridges across the tracks before, but not at stations. When the iron footbridges at the stations were introduced, some of the earlier wooden footbridges were replaced by iron ones as well.

Some of the first platforms were also made from wood, with the result that they became slippery in wet weather and though they were cheap to erect, they decayed quickly. Therefore, they were soon replaced with stone platforms. Again, in the beginning, these platforms were quite short, as were the trains. Soon more passengers used the line, the trains got longer and the platforms had to be extended accordingly, a procedure that went on right into the twenty-first century.

Railway stations/stops of the D&KR and the DART and times they were open[16]

D&KR	open	open	open	open	DART	open
					Grand Canal Dock	2001–
Serpentine Ave	1835 (2 m★)				–	
Lansdowne Rd	1870–1984				Lansdowne Rd	1984–
Sandymount	1835–1841	1860-62	1882–1901	1928–60	Sandymount	1984–
Sydney Parade	1835–1841	1862-1960			Sydney Parade	1984–
Merrion	1835–1860	1882–1901	1928-9★★	1930-35	–	
Booterstown	1835–1960				Booterstown	1984–
Williamstown	1835–1841				–	
Blackrock	1834–1984				Blackrock	1984–
Seapoint	1837–1960				Seapoint	1984–
Salth.&Monkst.	1837–1960				Salth.&Monkst.	1984–

2 m★ two months only
★★ according to other sources open from 1928 until 1933

Sandymount Halt has a special historical event all of its own. Despite the fact that it was officially closed between 1841 and 1860, it became famous in 1849 when Queen Victoria visited Ireland for the first time. The royal party arrived by boat at Kingstown (Dún Laoghaire) Harbour and thence proceeded in a special train to Sandymount, where a platform had been erected especially for this visit. The royals and their attendants left the train there and made their way from Sandymount Avenue through Ballsbridge into Dublin in carriages.

In 1863, *Bradshaw's Handbook* says of the stretch from Kingstown to Dublin:

> After traversing the Dublin and Kingstown railway, and stopping at the stations Salthill, Blackrock, Booterstown, and Merrion, we arrive at Dublin.[17]

The first track of the Dublin & Kingstown Railway line was built in the gauge of 1,435mm (4ft 8½in), which is now known as the standard (or international) gauge. When the line was extended via Dalkey to Bray and later to Wicklow and finally Wexford and Rosslare Harbour, the gauge was changed to what is now known as the Irish gauge of 1,600mm (5ft 3in).

Originally, tickets could only be bought for the whole stretch and were priced according to class and not distance. There were three classes. Some publications insist that there were four classes, but the railway company did not price tickets for the open second-class differently from those in the closed second-class carriages. Open second-class carriages were only used during the summer months. Later, different types of tickets were introduced, which might have been an incentive for the passengers to use the railway, but did not make it easier for a clerk selling tickets.

K.A. Murray reports that in 1842 no fewer than forty-seven different tickets, with, of course, different prices, were available.[18] Prices were different for the three classes, both for adults and children, both single and return; there were ticket books of ten tickets, seasonal tickets for three different lengths of time (one month, six months or one year), all with reductions in case a member of the same family bought an additional seasonal ticket. There were also two different types of combined tickets for return journeys, including the use of the baths run by the railway company. Murray states that it would have been possible to get from Dublin to Blackrock, have a quick swim and get the return train back to the city, all within just one hour.[19]

And then there were 'morning tickets', which were tickets that were reduced in price for people who used the train in the early morning between six and seven o'clock and perhaps again late in the evening to return. Those tickets were greatly in demand for workmen of Dublin firms who went to work in the suburbs early in the morning and returned to town late in the evening. They were also used in the other direction by hawkers, travelling salesmen, who went to town early in the morning to stock up on the wares that they then sold during the day, walking around the suburbs.

Another type of ticket was introduced for people who walked along the strand, beside the railway, until they got tired and took the train from the next station to the terminus, refreshed themselves there and then went back home by train.

Magistrates, the Dublin Metropolitan Police and the criminals the policemen escorted all had special rates. Dogs had to pay as well. An old story explains that it was not always clear whether dogs were the only animals that had to pay. A ticket clerk, when asked if it was necessary to buy a dog ticket for a tortoise, responded: 'Cats is dogs and rabbitses is dogs, but tortoises is hinsects and goes free.'

Rolling Stock

The first six locomotives that the Dublin & Kingstown Railway Company bought were made by different firms; three were built by George Forrester & Company, Vauxhall Foundry, Liverpool, and had the names *Dublin*, *Kingstown* and *Vauxhall*. The other three were built by Sharp Brothers of Manchester and were named *Hibernia*, *Britannia* and *Manchester*. The best-known and most often depicted locomotive is the *Hibernia*.

It seems unlikely that the engraver understood the mechanism of a locomotive as this one cannot have worked as it is depicted. The forward- and backward-moving 'N' lever reaches down outside the framework of the locomotive with the platform on which the engineman stands. It is connected with the 'O' rod, which is supposed to transform the forward and

LOCOMOTIVE ENGINE—DUBLIN AND KINSTOWN RAILWAY.

Locomotive *Hibernia* by Sharp Brothers, Manchester. Engraved by Robert Clayton.

backward motion into a rotary motion. To do this, it is fixed to the drive wheel, which, however, is shown to turn on the inside of the framework. This is simply not possible as the edge of the framework would smash the 'O' rod before the drive wheel could have done even a half-turn. Astonishingly, quite a few of the early engravings of locomotives make the same mistake.

A description of the Dublin and Kingstown Railway was published in 1834 by P. Dixon Hardy, both in his paper, *Penny Journal*, and in a separate brochure, but this was quite obviously produced before the building of the line was completed and the trains were running, as some of the descriptions do not fit the reality of the railway. His brochure shows a train on the line roughly at Merrion, with Howth in the background, and mentions carriages of first, second, third and fourth class. The Dublin & Kingstown Railway Company only mentions first, second and third class in their price list for tickets. The discrepancy might be explained by the fact that there was an open second class and a closed second class, the former with carriages that were partly open. The ticket prices for both were the same, though, as they depended on the number of seats per carriage. In the beginning, trains were usually composed of one first-class carriage, two second-class carriages and three third-class carriages; later they might have had one first-class, four second-class and three third-class carriages.

A Dublin and Kingstown train at Merrion, with Howth in the background.

First-class carriages held three passengers per seat row on stuffed cushions, with eighteen passengers per carriage. Those carriages also had blinds on the windows. Second-class carriages held four passengers per seat row and twenty-four per carriage. They were obviously less luxurious than first class, but still had seats that were upholstered, though some of them (not used in winter) were open from waist-level up. Those carriages could hold twenty-eight passengers. Third-class carriages were open from waist-level up as well and they did not even have doors. They had seats of uncovered boards and low back-rests, took five passengers per seat row and thirty-five passengers per carriage all in all. Despite what is shown in contemporary prints, it also has to be said that all D&KR carriages had roofs.

The carriages were colour-coded and so were the tickets, in order to help passengers find their carriage. First-class carriages were purple, closed second-class pale yellow, open second-class green and third-class carriages were blue.[20]

Some of the carriages showed a great similarity in design to horse-drawn coaches, as seen in an engraving of an early second-class carriage, which gives the impression of three mail coaches put side by side onto a railway carriage chassis.

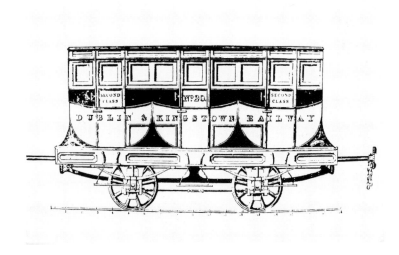

Second-class railway carriage of the D&KR.

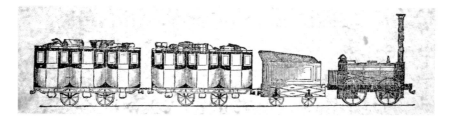

Railway train. Illustration from the first Brockhaus edition, 1837.

In a picture used in a BBC series about railways, a very similar-looking carriage is described as 'A model of the multiple-body railway coach used on the Liverpool and Manchester Railway, 1834',[21] indicating that early railway carriages had more or less the same look, at least in Britain and Ireland, regardless of the company which used them. The roof of the carriages often carried the luggage, as evidenced in an illustration in the first *German Encyclopaedia* by F.A. Brockhaus, which was published in 1837.[22]

As the carriages in this illustration look very much like the picture of a second-class carriage of the D&KR, it is possible that the illustration shows an Irish or English train. It is also possible that the carriages of the first German railway (1835) were modelled on English or Irish carriages.

From the beginning of the railway until the early 1960s, railway trains were pulled by steam engines. Driving the very early locomotives seems to have necessitated something between craft, art and wizardry, as the railway engineer William Richard Le Fanu, younger brother of the writer Joseph Sheridan Le Fanu, describes in an anecdote:

Father H—— told me that he had got into a second-class carriage one night by the last train leaving Dublin for Bray. Before the train started a woman, whose name he could not remember, but whom he recognizes as a parishioner, came to the door and said, 'Father James, have you any objection to my coming in here?' 'Not in the least,' said he. So in she came, and sat on the seat opposite to him. Off went the train at such a pace as he had never known before; it jumped and swayed from side to side. Father H—— was naturally much alarmed. The woman, observing this, said to him, 'Don't be the least uneasy, Father James. Sure it's my Jim that's driving; and when he has a dhrop taken, it's him that can make her walk.'[23]

Some of the early steam engines could be surprisingly fast. When, in February 1835, the parliament in Westminster elected a new speaker, Dublin's *Evening Mail* had made special arrangements to get the results as quickly as possible as the new speaker would have a great influence on politics for Ireland during the coming years and the two candidates had very different views regarding Ireland. After the vote, the result got to Holyhead by relays of riders and was then communicated by signalling to a ship, which crossed the Irish Sea despite a storm. As soon as the boat was in sight of Kingstown Harbour, signal flags went up, the result was passed to the fastest engine the railway company had and was brought to Dublin in nine minutes.[24] To compare: according to the 2016 timetable, the shortest time by the Dublin to Rosslare Harbour Intercity on that stretch, without any stop, is fourteen minutes from Dún Laoghaire to Dublin and eleven minutes from Dublin to Dún Laoghaire. It should be remembered, though, that the 1835 engine had no train to pull and at those times the security measures were much lower than they are nowadays. Still, the 1835 engine managed an average speed of 66km/h (41mph).

As far as security was concerned, both for people and for the rolling stock, D&KR company rules held that no engine should be left unattended. As in other times, rules in those years were not always stuck to. In summer 1844, a director driving along Merrion Road discovered an unattended locomotive at Merrion Gates. Stopping his carriage for a further inspection of this surprising situation, he encountered the crew returning from the Coach and Horses inn, where they had refreshed themselves with cider, probably driven there by a very dusty and dirty job. It is not known, however, whether a possible delay was announced ('… will be late for operational reasons' or perhaps '… is delayed due to a late incoming train'?).

Later, the carriages became longer, but each compartment had its own door, still with a window on each side of the door, obviously a relic from the old coach days and the first railway carriages in the 1830s. The photograph shows a train meeting the mail boat after a branch had been built from the main line northwards onto Carlisle Pier, where the mail boats docked.

The steam locomotives then looked different from the first ones, still old-fashioned to our eyes, but much more modern compared with the first steam locomotive on the line, the *Hibernia*. Neither the D&KR, nor its successor the D&SER, ever had the most modern, streamlined steam locomotives. Their trains looked endearingly rural (see Plate 3). The old postcard clearly states, 'Dublin and South-Eastern Railway', but no stretch of this rail line is outside a built-up area and still has that many tracks.

Train meeting the mail boat on Carlisle Pier, 1920s; from an old postcard.

There are no more steam engines in regular use today, but some have been preserved and restored to full working order and are mainly used for pulling trains of restored old carriages on the main line for both railway enthusiasts and families with kids. Steam trains work all year round and there are many at Christmas time, with Santa on board.

The steam engine in the photograph, which will go on to collect some carriages and puff off as the Santa Express, is K 2 class 2-6-0 No. 461, which was built by Beyer, Peacock & Co., Manchester, in 1922, works number 6112. She first served as D&SER 15 from 1922, pulling goods trains on the Dublin to Wexford line. Later, when the D&SER was absorbed into the GSR in 1925, she was renumbered as 461 and continued working with goods and beet trains until 1962.

Charles P. Friel of the RPSI kindly provided the following information about the locomotive:

Rather than being cut up, Córas Iompair Éireann announced in 1967 that No 461 would be one of three preserved steam locomotives on display at various

Steam engine 461 at Pearse Station, December 2014.

stations on the network. No 461 was repainted in DSER lined black livery for the 1968 Inchicore Open Day and, rather than go on display at Wexford as planned, the loco remained at Inchicore until it was moved to Cork loco shed for storage. The loco was acquired outright by the Railway Preservation Society of Ireland (RPSI) in 1967 and moved to the Society's base in Mullingar. Following a move to the Society headquarters at Whitehead, county Antrim, the loco underwent a heavy overhaul by the Society's volunteers. As part of the locomotive's restoration to main line condition, many new parts had to be made to replace those lost during her years of inactivity. The loco made its first trial run on the main line on 22 August 1990. There followed many running-in trips which involved the loco hauling passenger trains to Larne, Bangor, Coleraine and Dundalk. Then, on 16 April 1991, the loco was officially launched by the President Mrs Mary Robinson at Pearse Station and then worked a Presidential Special to Dún Laoghaire for a reception.

In the years which followed, there was little of the Irish railway system which the loco did not visit with various RPSI special trains to Portrush, Mullingar,

Westport, Ballina, Limerick, Foynes, Galway, Cork, Cobh, Sligo, Tralee, Waterford, Kilkenny, Ennis, and Nenagh, for instance.

The loco was also been a frequent visitor to its home line (south of Pearse) and has worked many recreations of the past with 'Sea Breeze' specials to Bray, Greystones, Wicklow and Rosslare Harbour. The loco has also appeared in several cinema films and television programmes. No 461 hauled another Presidential Special on 18 October 2010 when President Mrs Mary McAleese officially launched GSWR Royal Saloon No 351 which had been fully restored to its 1903 splendour by the RPSI at Inchicore Works – and there was another Presidential Special to a reception at Dún Laoghaire!

A steam locomotive has to be stopped every 10 years for a heavy overhaul, so No 461 worked back to Whitehead in early 2001 and remained there, with much work ongoing, until November 2011. The work needed on her firebox, for instance, was quite extensive.

Towards the end of that overhaul, the loco's battleship grey livery was replaced with the lined green livery which CIÉ applied to many passenger locomotives in 1947. No 461 had not been one of them but the Society felt that the loco deserved something better than plain grey and, maybe, it should have been painted green in 1947!

Since her 2001 restoration, the loco has again been mostly based in Dublin and has revisited many parts of the IÉ system. This time she has added M3 Parkway, Howth and Midleton to her list of achievements, has worked many specials including, of course, many Santa specials. Just about the only place left unvisited, so far, is Derry/Londonderry Waterside!

No 461 is the only survivor of the former Dublin and South Eastern Railway, is the only inside-motion 2-6-0 preserved in these islands, and is one of very few locomotives to have retained its original tender all the way into preservation.

On the day those photographs were taken, it was more grown men than children who inspected the now unusual machine and pointed things out to each other. It was not long, however, before they jumped back from a sudden emission of steam when she went to collect her carriages while a diesel-electric multiple unit arrived on another track.

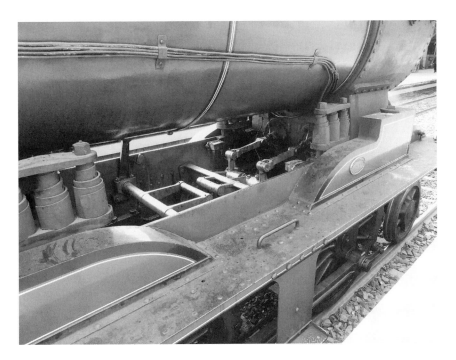

Steam engine 461, detail.

As her 'face mask' showed, on this day, she puffed off to collect carriages of several different types, which would then be combined to form the Santa Express, which would collect families with kids, as well, in many cases as the children in the men (Plate 4).

Most of the carriages shown in Plate 4 (except the first one) belong to the stock built completely or in part by Cravens in Sheffield and were in use from 1963 to 2006. Carriages that were delivered only part-finished were completed by CIÉ in Inchicore. Those carriages were in use on the stretch from Dublin to Arklow into the twenty-first century. Later carriages were more modern, but looked similar. The livery used at that stage by CIÉ (black around the windows and medium brown below) was kept until 1988, when white stripes separated black and brown. Cream and blue is the livery of the RPSI. Very early CIÉ carriages were green.

DART users occasionally discover some of those trains that have been put together by the Railway Preservation Society for special trips, which are usually booked out long in advance.

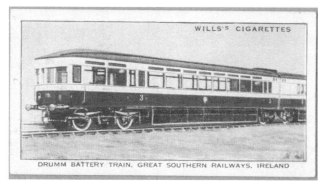

Craven carriage of the first generation (1963–2006).

Drumm battery train; from a cigarette card.

Before these carriages were in service, a completely different system was used. For some years from 1932 on, battery-driven railcars with rechargeable batteries were in use on the stretch between Amiens Street (now Connolly) Station and Bray. The batteries were designed by James Drumm and so the trains were called Drumm trains after him. They had first-class and third-class compartments, but no second-class. Drumm trains were very useful during the 'Emergency' as they needed neither coal nor diesel. After some time, more modern Drumm railcars ran nearly exclusively on the Harcourt Street to Bray line.

When the batteries used in those railcars reached the end of their life, CIÉ decided not to order any more batteries as, at that stage, cheap diesel was available and diesel-driven railcars were introduced instead.

In the early 1950s, after the Drumm trains had come to the end of their service, CIÉ bought multi-unit push-pull diesel-electric railcars of the 2600 class. The expression 'push-pull' means that even though the engine might have been just at one end of the unit, the unit could go in either direction without having to be turned; the engine, wherever it was, could push the unit or pull it. Those units could have between two and eight carriages, with a maximum of four engine-carriages. These diesel-powered trains were not very satisfactory and later had to be driven by a CIÉ 201 class locomotive on one end, but could be controlled from a driver's cabin in a carriage on the other end, so that they could still be pulled or pushed. The carriages that were rebuilt as driver trailers were also renumbered.

By the late 1970s, the need for an urgent upgrade of the system had become apparent as the 2600 class railcars were in poor condition. Replacement

Push-pull diesel-electric rail cars, 2600 class, 1974. © Albert Bridge.

Diesel locomotive of the 201 class, pulling a freight train out of Pearse Station, 2003.

parts had become increasingly difficult to obtain due to the age of the rolling stock. The push-pull operation, which had been intended as a temporary measure until a more permanent solution could be established, had come to the end of its serviceable life.[25] The depicted railcar with the number 6111 had been converted to a push-pull driving trailer in 1974 (former number 2624). It was acquired by the Downpatrick & County Down Railway in 2015 and will be overhauled there.[26]

In the early 1950s, CIÉ had started to phase out steam locomotives, partly because of the need to modernise the old material, but also because coal had grown scarcer and oil became easier to source. Some steam engines were still used in the 1960s, though.

One of the earlier types of diesel locomotives was the 201 class, which was built in the mid-1950s by Metropolitan-Vickers in Manchester. Originally they were meant for branch-line traffic. When many branch lines were closed, they got new engines and were used for freight trains and later also for short commuter trains. They were officially withdrawn in the mid-1980s.

Until the mid-1980s, the railway stretch between Westland Row and Dún Laoghaire still saw regular traffic of goods trains, pulled by diesel locomotives like this:

Diesel locomotive of the 071 class in Pearse Station in 2010.

This is an engine of the 071 class which was built in 1976 by General Motors Electro-Motive Division. Originally meant for passenger trains, they were overhauled from 2013 onwards and are still in use on freight and permanent way trains. They have a very distinctive driver's cabin at the front and back.

Diesel locomotives were phased out for passenger trains and this service was gradually taken over by diesel-electric multiple unit trains. Originally different classes of those multiple units existed, but the only ones still going on the stretch that used to be the D&KR is the 29000 class, mainly for commuter trains, and the 22000 class, mainly but not exclusively for intercity trains.

The 29000 class multiple units have four parts. The photograph shows two of those units forming one train. This is the longest train possible on the line as the station platforms are not built to service longer trains.

Driver cabin of CIÉ locomotive 085 of the 071 class.

The 22000 class multiple units on this line are, in general, used for intercity trains to and from Rosslare Harbour via Wexford. Plate 5 shows one of them passing Sandymount Station, heading for Pearse. Lately, some of them can be seen at the Grand Canal Dock Station, which serves as the terminus for commuter trains to Drogheda or Newbridge. Those units can have three, four or five sections, depending on the expected number of passengers. The train shown in Plate 5 has four units. The longest trains of that type seen on this stretch are trains of two multiple units, one with four sections and the other with three. Any longer combination would exceed the length of the existing platforms.

In 1960, the service for most of the stops between Westland Row and Dún Laoghaire had been discontinued and for twenty-four years any commuter on that stretch would have to rely on the bus service. In the early 1980s, a stretch from Howth through Dublin City centre to Bray was electrified and a new commuter service was introduced, the Dublin Area Rapid Transit, which is known to everybody in Dublin as the DART. From 1984 on, electric multiple units were used for the stretch from Howth to Bray. Later the line was extended to the north to Malahide and to the south to Greystones.

Multiple unit 29000 class passing Sandymount Stop, 2017.

Older DART unit (8100 class), leaving Grand Canal Dock Station travelling towards Bray, 2017.

DART unit of the 8200 class at Grand Canal Dock Station. © Keith Edkins

Double four-carriage unit of the DART 8520 class leaving Sandymount northwards, 2017.

8500 class DART, 29000 class and 22000 class diesel-electric units at Grand Canal Dock, 2017.

The first electric units of the 8100 class were two carriage units, which could be coupled with one or more other units of that type. In the beginning, trains with one, two or three units were used. Units of this class are still on duty. Units of the 8200 class were only on duty between 2000 and 2008. Those units were two-carriage units also. They could be connected to another two-carriage unit of their class, but also to two-carriage units of the 8100 class.

As the number of passengers was constantly increasing, trains with eight carriages were being considered, but before they could be introduced, the platforms had to be changed. Until the first years of the twenty-first century, platforms on this, as on most other lines, were long enough only for six-carriage trains. After the extension of platforms was achieved in the early 2000s, the newest electric four-carriage units of the 8500/8510/8520 class could be used, even when two of them were coupled together.

Sometimes two or more multi-carriage units of different types and ages meet at or near a station, *en route*, in transit or starting service.

Explanation Concerning Steam Locomotive Classification

There are different ways to classify steam engines. The classification which is most common in Britain and Ireland is the Whyte notation, which describes the number of wheels. The wheels of a steam locomotive, however, have different functions. The important ones are the driving wheels. Wheels before them are called leading wheels and the wheels after the driving wheels are called trailing wheels. The classification of steam locomotives gives the number of wheels in the sequence: leading wheels, driving wheels, trailing wheels. The *Hibernia* would be described as a 2-2-0 locomotive, or sometimes just as a 2-2, as most of the early locomotives did not have any trailing wheels.

The abovementioned steam engine 461 is described as a 2-6-0 engine, which means that she has two leading wheels, six driving wheels and no trailing wheels. When describing the changes in the line, another steam engine is shown, passing the old Booterstown Station. This is engine no. 186, which is a 0-6-0 locomotive. In other words, she has six driving wheels and neither leading nor trailing wheels.

In many other countries, steam locomotives are classified according to the UIC system, which does not count the wheels, but the axles. Axles of driven wheels are described with capital letters. The *Hibernia*, in this system, would be a 1A locomotive, engine 461 would be classified as 1C and engine 186 would be a C engine. In this system, there are additional signs to describe additional properties: for instance, if leading and/or trailing axles are mounted on a bogie, an apostrophe would follow the number of axles involved. According to this system, most German steam locomotives for express trains were classified as 2'C 1', which would, according to Whyte notation, be 4-6-2.

Manpower

The line was built manually. No machinery was used. Even before the great famine between 1845 and 1849, the situation of the Irish lower classes was appalling. In the early 1830s, there were very few jobs for the poor. On top of that, cholera broke out in 1832 and 1833 in the Dublin area. Ringsend, Irishtown and Sandymount were very badly affected by it. Building the railway should have been a godsend to those people, but they were so emaciated that the railway company ignored them and employed people from the countryside as they were stronger and thus better able to survive the hard manual work.

The working day was long and the wages were rather low, even for those times. In general, there were no paid holidays, no sick pay, no pension and no social security at all. Gatemen at level crossings employed by the D&KR in its early years worked a twelve-hour day for 10s a week. An engineman (driver) often had more than one eighteen-hour day each week and on days on which he worked shorter hours driving the engine, he spent quite a number of hours in the workshop, keeping his engine in order, checking, cleaning and even repairing it. The average work week was 90 hours and could even rise to 110 hours. As trains stopped at termini for only a short time and the engine had to be turned during that time, enginemen and firemen hardly had time to eat or even drink during their shifts, despite the fact that it was very thirsty work.

No wonder irregularities sometimes occurred, like the instance in 1844, mentioned above, when a railway company director, who did not use the railway himself but drove along Merrion Road, noticed an unattended locomotive near Merrion Gates – something that was strictly forbidden. It is not reported what he said to the crew when he discovered them coming out of the Coach and Horse inn near Merrion Castle, where they had tried to quench their thirst with cider. They were fined, but at least they were not dismissed.

In the mid-nineteenth century, it was customary to tip anybody who had done somebody a service. For some reason, accepting tips was officially forbidden by the D&KR company. As the wages were so low, it is not surprising that many of the railway employees did accept tips, despite the rules and bylaws.

Not only was there no sick pay in general for the lowest-paid employees in any company; when an employee did not report for work for whatever reason, his colleagues had to do his work, on top of their own. The D&KR company seems to have been better than other companies, as there was some kind of sick pay for clerks and workers of the D&KR and the company had an arrangement with the City of Dublin Hospital on Baggot Street and also the Rathdown (later Monkstown) Hospital in Monkstown, both of which provided medical help for D&KR employees. This might have been the reason why many employees of the D&KR would not even think of changing to another company: other railway companies might have paid higher wages, but they did not do anything for their employees during illness or even after work accidents.

Altogether, the D&KR employed men as station keepers, ticket clerks, ticket collectors, parcel clerks, enginemen (drivers), firemen (stokers), guards, assistant guards, pointsmen, watchmen, policemen and porters.[27] Surely there were other roles also, as the 1901 census records the following professions for people living in Railway Cottages beside the railway, just south of Lansdowne Station: plate layer, railway labourer, ticket collector, railway porter, office boy, railway signalman, railway station master, assistant station master, railway clerk and railway servant. For 1911, the list reads: railway ganger, railway storeman, railway inspector, railway ticket checker, railway signalman, railway employee, railway servant, railway ticket collector, railway goods checker and railway plate layer. It is highly likely that many readers will not be familiar with the expressions 'plate layer' or 'ganger'. A plate layer is somebody who inspects and maintains the rails and sleepers (which, as a whole, is called the permanent way) of a railway line. Plate layers usually work in groups or gangs. The headman of the group is the railway ganger. There are still railway employees who work as plate layers and gangers, though the description of their job might be different now. They are usually only seen near level crossings. Occasionally one still hears the 'ganger's' horn warning his gang that a train is approaching.

The *House of Commons Papers*, 1856, volume 4 gives the following information about employees of the Dublin & Kingstown Railway for June 1856:

Secretaries or Managers	1
Treasurers	1
Engineers	2
Superintendants	4
Storekeepers	1
Accountants or Cashiers	2
Inspectors or Timekeepers	1
Station Masters	5
Ticket Collectors	8
Draughtsmen	1
Clerks	6
Foremen	3
Engine Drivers	8
Assistant Engine Drivers or Firemen	9
Guards or Brakesmen	9
Artificers	51
Switchmen	4
Gatekeepers	12
Policemen or Watchmen	18
Porters or Messengers	39
Platelayers	12
Labourers	40[28]

The biggest group of employees is described using the old-fashioned word 'artificer'. Today this word is used for skilled mechanics in the armed forces. Originally it meant any skilled craftsman.

The above table gives a total of 237 employees for a line that, at that time, had a length of 6 miles and 7 chains (9.8 km). The paper also mentions that the line had six stations. Other sources state that there were seven stations (including the termini) at that time. It is possible that the paper only counted the stations the train stopped at after starting to move.

Something has to be said about the term 'engineer' as this term describes different positions in different contexts and/or areas. In the language of the United States, the word 'engineer' in the early days of railways describes what in the early days of the D&KR was called the 'engine man'. This later changed to 'engine driver'. The assistant engine driver had been called the 'fireman' in the early days. Later the fireman was described as the 'stoker'. As the table of employees lists engineers separate to engine drivers, the word 'engineer' on this list must describe a superior position, as there were just two of them in the company, whereas there were eight engine drivers. 'Engineer' must have been used to indicate a position that could be described as a technical supervisor or even a technical director nowadays. Charles Blacker Vignoles, for instance, who planned the railway, was regarded as the railway engineer of the line.

Changes on the Line

The easiest way to detect changes on a railway line is to walk on, or at least beside, the line. During the first years of the D&KR, walking on the line was actually allowed in certain cases and for some stretches: for instance, in the case of poor fishermen who found that walking on the line was the easiest way to get to a stretch of the strand where they dug for bait. This was especially true of the stretches where the railway had been built on a causeway across parts of the bay, e.g. the stretch between Merrion and Seapoint. Today, walking on any railway line is forbidden, of course, and on the stretch of the former D&KR would be highly dangerous, considering the number of trains using the line and the fact that electric and diesel-electric trains make much less noise than the earlier steam engines did. The steam engines could be heard approaching from quite a distance away. The next best way of detecting changes is to walk on official paths or streets beside the tracks. Unluckily, on the stretch that used to be the D&KR, that is only possible for around half the distance between the two former termini.

The Elevated Stretch

In Dublin 2 and the northern part of Dublin 4, there are some stretches where streets – mostly cul-de-sacs – run directly parallel to the railway line, but as the railway is elevated on this stretch, nothing much could be seen from those streets except a tall wall, with the trains rattling past the first floor or even higher than the rooftops of the houses on the other side of the narrow street.

But let's start at what was once the beginning of the line.

Railway Terrace, south of
the railway and west of
Macken Street, 2017.

Westland Row

The first and most obvious change here is that, even though the main entrance is still accessed from Westland Row, the station is no longer called Westland Row. The street on its north side is not called Great Brunswick Street any more either. The street was renamed Pearse Street in 1923 and the station was renamed Pearse Station in 1966. Many Dubliners still refer to it as Westland Row, though.

According to a plan of Westland Row Station after alterations in early 1835,[29] it then had two halls and a total of five tracks and four platforms. The counting of the four platforms seems to have been from south to north, from 1 to 4, with a fifth track on the north side of the station described in the plan as 'spare line of rails (siding)'. In the early 1990s, the two platforms still in use were numbered from south to north still, with platform 3 serving the northbound trains and platform 4 serving the southbound ones.

By 2000, Pearse Station had become a bit tired-looking, with rust everywhere. A metal fence on the north side of the southbound platform blocked off track 5 (then still in existence), with its own platform, which

Pearse Station from the south in 2003.

The remaining four tracks from the eastern end of Pearse Station, 2017.

would have been platform 5; however, in the first years of the twenty-first century, this platform was no longer in use.

When looking out of the eastern end of Pearse Station, four tracks can be seen, even at the time of writing, in 2017. A fifth track, the one that has been replaced with a car park, would have been where a ramp now leads to the car park. That should have been track 1, according to the old counting. Tracks 2 and 5 are still there, but do not reach the station hall any more, though a short bit of an old platform can still be seen on what was originally track 5.

The roof over the two halls was partly built according to plans by Richard Turner of Hammersmith Ironworks in Ballsbridge.

Large numbers of pigeons in the big hall did not improve the overall impression, especially when they roosted on the iron girders under the curved roof and dirtied the station with their droppings. Nets were introduced to try to protect passengers from the numerous pigeons and look like clouds in the hall. It seems that the number of pigeons has decreased since those nets were put up, but there are still quite a few of them around.

Roof of Pearse
Station, 2017.

The Victorian ironwork that holds up the roof has maintained its old charm. Luckily, neither the brick walls nor the iron construction were changed during the later renovations and upgrading of the station, though the brickwork has been cleaned and the ironwork de-rusted and painted, as seen in Plate 6.

The brick walls of the late nineteenth century might look old-fashioned, but they create a much warmer impression than modern concrete would. Even an old drainpipe at the end of the brick wall is still there, albeit with a later overflow pipe leading from it. Perhaps the authorities should consider putting a warning notice on the platform under that overflow pipe, as it allows water to drop down on any passenger who inadvertently stands under it.

A major change introduced during the restructuring of the station resulted in the second, smaller hall not being used for trains at all any more and the two platforms in that hall have disappeared. The counting seems to have been from the oldest, now disappeared, platform, as in the 1990s the platform for northbound trains (now platform 1) was still called platform 3 and today's platform 2 was then platform 4.

Platforms 1 and 2 (by the old numbering) were located in the southern, narrower and shorter station hall and were meant for trains that terminated at Westland Row. They seem to have been the original platforms from 1834.

The two station halls of Pearse Station seen from the south, 2015.

The smaller of the two halls of Westland Row Station, north end, 2017.

One of the former platforms was used only occasionally and the other former platform was not suitable for modern trains and was therefore removed.

During the first years of the twenty-first century, it was still possible to look down onto the houses on Erne Terrace Rear (Plate 7). After the size of platform 2 was changed and big office blocks were built beside the station, this was no longer possible. Unlike other little streets directly beside the railway further east, Erne Terrace Rear is not a cul-de-sac, but the trains that pass the houses there pass on tracks that lie considerably higher even than the rooftops of the cottages. Life in those houses must be quite claustrophobic, with the railway high up on one side and tall modern office blocks on the western end. There is no space to park a car either, but perhaps the authorities are of the opinion that people living beside a railway station and near bus stops are unlikely to rely on a private car and consequently unlikely to own one.

Before the office blocks were built, the space between the eastern end of the station hall and Pearse Street was used as a car park. When inspecting the

Car park in the old smaller hall, 2017.

Car park between Pearse Street and Pearse Station, 2005.

station building from the street on the other side of this car park, it was easy to see that a renovation of Pearse Station was necessary.

Ten years later, the car park had disappeared and it is no longer possible to see whether the brickwork of Pearse Station is still sooty on the outside. A big concrete-and-glass office block was constructed where the car park had been, as well as a new second entrance to the station. Today, from more or less the same viewpoint from which the car park was seen, an office block can be seen.

Perhaps the biggest change is how the station has grown. Plate 8 shows an engraving by John Harris Jr of one of the first trains leaving Westland Row terminus in 1834. The drawing of the locomotive and the engine driver might not be quite right, but note the size of the station in the picture. As the station is shown on the left, the view must be eastwards. At that stage, Cumberland Street was obviously east of the station and the bridge across it began after the end of the station. This is confirmed by a look at the 1843 OS map, which shows clearly that the building which this map describes as

Office block with Pearse Street entrance to Pearse Station, 2017.

'Decorated' remains of former water filling point.

'Railroad Station Ho.' does not yet reach across Cumberland Street South, but has its eastern end on the west side of this street.

Not far east of the former Westland Row Station, on the southern side of the tracks, another relic of the steam-engine era is still standing, at least in parts. This is the water tank, which replenished the water supply of the steam engines.

This is of no use, of course, either for diesel-electric or for electric multiple units. Instead, as can be seen, graffiti artists find it to be a useful panel on which to display their art to passing railway passengers. It is not the only place where graffiti of varying quality can be seen by DART passengers.

Bridges

Plate 8 shows an early picture of Cumberland Street Bridge. The workmen who are depicted beside the station are still busily working on St Andrew's church, which has its main entrance on Westland Row. The church was built in the years between 1832 and 1837.[30]

Compared with the 1843 map, the 1912 map shows great changes. The station building has been greatly expanded to the east and south, so that from then on and still in the twenty-first century, Cumberland Street is no longer behind the eastern end of the station, but under it. As the whole station has not only been lengthened, but also widened, the arch of the bridge can only be detected in the middle of the bridge.

The photograph shows both the widening and the lengthening of the station, as the rounded roof built in 1884 stretches across Cumberland Street.

This widening of the station and consequently the bridge over Cumberland Street makes crossing under it a bit eerie, as John E. Mullee writes in his recollection of the early 1950s:

> The cavernous railway bridge under Westland Row station always made me feel like I was in a tunnel. Whatever daylight entered the tunnel was quickly neutralized by dark limestone walls streaked with calcium seeps. These reminded me of chalk scribbles on a blackboard.[31]

This was one of the first bridges built. All the other bridges that were necessary were supposed to be much like this one, but the Wide Street Commissioners objected. They insisted that on either side of the thoroughfare

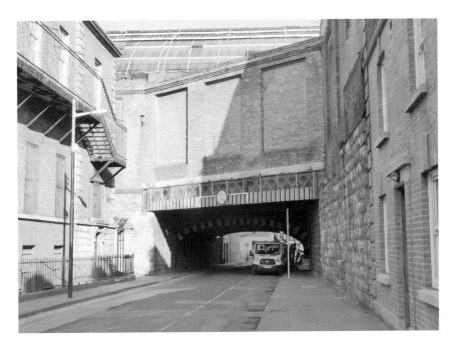

Cumberland Street Bridge under Pearse Station, 2017.

A train crossing South Sandwith Street in the mid-1830s, drawn by Jones, engraved by Clayton.

for cars there should be space for foot passengers to pass under the railway bridge without having to step onto the roadway. This is shown on a similar old engraving, this time of the South Sandwith Street Bridge. Occasionally those two pictures are mixed up and the picture of Cumberland Street is described as a picture of South Sandwith Street. As the Sandwith Street Bridge was definitely built with, and still has, the passages for pedestrians that Cumberland Street Bridge never had, it should be easy to tell them apart, especially as the picture of Sandwith Street shows the station much further to the left than the view from Cumberland Street.

The little boy who raises both arms, with his hat in his right hand, appears in both pictures, which might have caused the confusion. He is obviously a stock figure for engravers to enliven the foreground, as he appears in several pictures by different engravers.

This bridge shows the three arches, which are still there today, but the surrounding landscape is no longer as open as on the old picture. It is not quite as it was in the early nineteenth century either, as the track system leading into Pearse Station has been widened and the original three arches are met only after passing under a modern, straight, concrete part of the bridge.

Sandwith Street railway bridge, 2017.

Office block seen from Pearse Station, 2017.

To see that this really is a railway bridge near Pearse Station, one just has to compare the top of the office block in the upper left of the photograph with a photograph of the same office block taken from platform 2 of Pearse Station.

The photograph of this bridge shows that, like the bridge across Cumberland Street, the stretch under the railway on Sandwith Street is longer than it was originally. The bridge across Macken Street, on the other hand, still resembles the original plan. An early engraving depicts this bridge being built. At that time, today's Macken Street was still called Great Clarence Street.

The engraving does not depict the bridge as it is now and it is obvious that some artistic licence was taken. The view shown is to the north-east, otherwise it would not be possible to see the masts of the ships in the Grand Canal Basin. In the engraving, the narrow arches right and left of the central arch are the same height as the arch in the middle. None of the three-arch bridges ever looked like that. The rather rural scenery in the foreground, however, is confirmed by the 1843 OS map, which shows open land there. Today the area is densely built up.

The modern photograph clearly shows how much lower the arches for foot passengers are, compared to the central arch for carriages.

East of Macken Street, the area for the railway widens again, with sidings used up to the present day to park temporarily unused diesel-electric multiple units. These sidings end near Grand Canal Quay. Some of them are already shown on the 1912 OS map. The older map of 1843 does not show them, but then this map does not show any sidings, not even going into what the map calls 'Railway Coach Factory'. The modern sidings, known as Boston Sidings, will not be used for much longer. A report in *The Irish Times* mentions that:

> the site had been used as sidings for train services for many years but would soon be no longer required for this purpose.[32]

According to this report, CIÉ is looking for partners with whom to develop the site for new office blocks.

The next bridge is not only low, but also narrow. As the street gave access to a number of firms that had goods delivered, the very low headroom clearance must have led to quite a few accidents.

View of the Kingstown Railroad where it crosses the street near the Docks at the Drawbridge, Ringsend.

Macken Street railway bridge, 2017.

Grand Canal Quay bridge, 2017.

Any cars colliding with a railway bridge cause a disturbance to the rail service because, after such an accident, a railway engineer has to certify that the bridge is still – or, after necessary repairs, again – safe to use. Despite this and the fact that those accidents occurred regularly, this bridge was only blocked for car traffic in the first years of the twenty-first century; it is now open only for cyclists and pedestrians. The bollards that block cars from passing are removable, which means that in special cases a car might be able to pass under the bridge. The maximum headroom of 2.36m (7ft 8in), however, is not enough for a modern ambulance.

Having crossed Grand Canal Quay, the Grand Canal Basin itself had to be spanned – it is over 100m (330ft) wide. As the railway does not intersect with it at a right angle, around 120m (395ft) of water had to be crossed. Building a bridge that long would have been expensive, so it was decided to build a causeway, with a bridge only at its western end. Both the OS map of 1843 and that of 1912 show the Grand Canal Basin still stretching south of the railway down to Maquay Bridge on Grand Canal Street. Now, nearly all of

Railway bridge over Grand Canal Basin, 2017.

Grand Canal Dock south of the railway has been landfilled and buildings have been erected on Grand Canal Plaza between the railway to the north, Grand Canal Street to the south, Barrow Street to the east and the last stretch of the Grand Canal to the west. This last remaining stretch of water is still crossed by an arched bridge, as shown in Plate 9.

Actually, a three-arch bridge was planned – and indeed also built – at the western end of the causeway. The first of the arches is used to bridge Grand Canal Quay, the third crosses the canal itself. The middle arch has disappeared under the Guinness malthouse and one end of the arch that crosses the canal is now hidden under that building.

The causeway supporting the railway across the northern end of the infill, or what used to be the southernmost part of the Grand Canal Basin, can still be seen from the MacMahon Bridge and Barrow Street, whereas the landfill with the buildings on it hides its other side.

From the start of the third millennium, the area around Grand Canal Basin was developed with the construction of many-storeyed office blocks for big

Railway line crossing Grand Canal Basin, 2017.

Grand Canal Dock Station, 2015.

international IT firms like Google and Facebook, as well as big accountancy and law firms. Consequently, it was decided to build a new station to serve their staff. The Grand Canal Dock Station was the first completely new station built on this stretch after the opening of the Lansdowne Road Station in 1870, when the railway was run by the D&SER. Grand Canal Dock Station was built for Iarnród Éireann, of course. Though the station itself has been built on land that had been reclaimed from a part of the Grand Canal Basin, the platform for southbound trains is constructed over the water of the Grand Canal Basin. Most likely for that reason, this station is not serviced during sports events or concerts in the nearby Aviva Stadium, as otherwise accidents caused by not very sober users of the DART waiting on the platform could occur.

From the beginning, this station had three platforms and it was later slightly changed with the result that some commuter trains going to Newbridge, Maynooth or Drogheda now start and terminate at Grand Canal Dock Station instead of Pearse Station, which is of benefit to all the office workers in the big firms around Grand Canal Dock.

View of Grand Canal Dock Station from the east side, 2015.

Railway Works at Grand Canal Street, 1902. © Harold Falye – Irish Railway Record Society, courtesy of Ciarán Cooney.

South of this new station, the 1843 OS map shows buildings described as 'Railway Coach Factory' and, on the equivalent map of 1912, as 'Railway Works D. & S. E. R.' These works were in use until 1925.

In 2006, a burnt-out building could still be seen from the north platform of the new station. On the 1912 OS map, this building has the words 'Engine Shed' beside it, but according to Ciarán Cooney of the Irish Railway Record Society (IRRS), it was the office/mess building for the locomotive staff.

Not long after this photograph was taken, the ruin was cleared away and the Montevetro building was erected on the spot. Looking down from the platform for southbound trains, one discovers a curious structure in which a lot of the rubbish that has been floating into the Grand Canal Basin ends up. Sometimes it is even possible to see Dublin wildlife working on this Dublin rubbish.

From Grand Canal Dock Station southwards, the railway line has two tracks only and it gradually sinks from its elevated site to ground level. But before ground level is reached, some more streets have to be crossed. The bridges crossing those streets consequently have to be rather low. Still, in the early years of the existence of trams, the (horse-drawn) tram no. 4 from

Burnt-out office/mess for the locomotive staff of the former D&SER Railway Works, 2006.

Swan and cygnets on nest made with rubbish, 2015.

Bath Avenue Bridge, looking westwards, 2011.

Nelson's Pillar to Sandymount Tower used double-decker tram cars that just barely managed to get through under the bridge at Bath Avenue, which gave rise to the famous quip attributed to Myles na gCopaleen:

> Gentlemen on the upper deck of a no. 4 tram cannot but be struck by the stonework of Bath Avenue Bridge.

Actually, the bridges on Barrow Street, South Lotts Road and Bath Avenue were so low that they were later rebuilt to make them more suitable for modern traffic. The railway could not be lifted, but the arches were replaced with straight concrete beams to keep the headroom at least of equal height across the whole width of the street.

The Flat Stretch on Land

As the level of the railway tracks was lowering gradually, when it came to the next road to be crossed, the tracks were no longer high enough above the ground for a bridge. When the line was built, this next stretch was still empty land. It stayed empty for decades, but that is not to say that it was not used. From 1873, most of the land north-east of the railway line was occupied by what was first called the Royal Park Stadium, a sports venue built by Henry Wallace Doveton Dunlop (1844–1930). During the development and enlarging of this stadium later, big stands were built, which extended over the railway line. At that stage, the stadium was already known as Lansdowne Road Stadium. Trains had to go under a part of the 'New West Stand', which was built in 1978 and demolished in 2007.

When the Lansdowne Road Stadium was taken down in 2007, some people expected that the new stadium would stay completely beside the railway line, but it was not to be.

It is true that there are no longer seats over the railway line, but the new stadium needed more entrances than the old one ever had and so, as the Shelbourne Road, Lansdowne Lane and Lansdowne Road entrances are reached from west of the railway, they use a platform that has been built over the railway tracks. While that platform was being built, there were quite a few weekends when no trains were travelling on this stretch to facilitate the building workers.

In 1834, some weeks before the actual opening, the *Penny Journal* described the line in this area, focusing especially on the solution to the problem of the tracks not being high enough for a bridge, but not quite low enough for an ordinary level crossing:

> The crossing at Haig's distillery is the first accessible point to the Railway from Dublin. This being but little frequented, the roadway has been raised by gentle approaches, and passes on the level of the Railroad.

The 'New' West Stand of Lansdowne Road Stadium as a roof for the railway line, 2006.

The railway line beside the Aviva Stadium, 2014.

Thus, we have come to the first of the five level crossings of the D&KR, which are all still in existence and in use today. Shortly after crossing Haig's Lane (now Lansdowne Road), the Dodder had to be crossed. The *Penny Journal* goes on to say:

> We next come to a handsome bridge of three arches across the river Dodder, with a side opening for foot passengers.[33]

This bridge was not only planned, but actually built. It was never really in use, though. Shortly before the railway line was supposed to be opened to the public, the Dodder swelled up in one of its many dangerous floods, uprooted trees and destroyed a wooden bridge further upriver. The debris damaged the new bridge in such a way that it was not possible to repair it. It might have looked a bit like London Bridge further down the Dodder, though most likely with narrower arches, as the Dodder is much narrower at the spot where the railway crosses it. London Bridge was built in 1857, not much more than twenty years later than the original railway bridge.

A temporary and provisional bridge had to be built within weeks. This was described on the 1843 OS map as 'Wooden Br.' This provisional bridge lasted longer than expected and was only replaced in 1847 by another wooden bridge and finally in 1851 by an iron structure, which again had to be repaired and strengthened a number of times because of flooding caused by the River Dodder. In 1934, it was replaced by the structure that is still in use today, though this has suffered in a number of later floods, in every case disturbing the rail traffic.

With all the rebuilding and repairs, the bridge has kept the separate arch for pedestrians walking along the Dodder. The platforms of Lansdowne Road Station extend over this bridge and the fence on the upriver side has been strengthened and raised to improve safety, whereas on the downriver

Railway bridge across the Dodder, 2010.

side the former fence was replaced not so long ago with a wall which makes it impossible to see the Dodder swinging north towards Ringsend either from the platform or from the train.

Plate 10 shows that when approaching this bridge from the Sandymount side, it is clear that the railway is not quite at the normal ground level yet. This approach also shows an archway from the path beside the railway, but lower than the tracks, to the path alongside the Dodder, as well as steps up to a footpath across the river on the railway bridge, running beside the railway, but separate from the tracks, of course.

Stretching from the level crossing at Lansdowne Road (formerly Haig's Lane) south-eastwards towards Sandymount is Lansdowne Road Station. This station was only opened in 1870 and it looks as if the station building in red-brown brick erected at the time has not been changed.

The current access from Lansdowne Road is a modern path leading to the entrance of the old building west of the tracks. This building gives access to the northbound platform.

Lansdowne Road Station building, north end, 2006.

The southbound platform still has one of the old signal boxes on its northern end beside the Lansdowne Road level crossing. It still contains a number of the levers with which signals were changed, as well as one of the huge wheels to close the gates on the level crossing in the times before barriers that could be lowered and raised were installed. This wheel was a big improvement from the times when the guard had to come out of his hut and open and close the gates by hand.

From the Dodder towards Sandymount, the path runs between the railway tracks on one side and Marian College on the other side. In this area, the newest installation on this path comes into sight: floodgates that can be closed in case of any possible flooding of the River Dodder. Further on, after those floodgates, on the stretch going south-east towards Sandymount, there used to be what K.A. Murray called an 'Engine Hospital'.[34] Here, for a year after delivery, the firms that had built and delivered locomotives to the D&KR had stationed a foreman with assistants and tools for the maintenance of their locomotives. Two firms were involved: Sharp Brothers of Manchester, who had delivered the *Hibernia*, for example, and George

Lansdowne Road Station building from the southbound platform, 2006.

Plate 1: Façade of Westland Row Station with Loop Line Bridge, 2017.

Plate 2: Dún Laoghaire (Mallin) Station, 2011.

Plate 3: A D&SER train on an old postcard.

Plate 4: Steam engine 461 and old railway carriages in different liveries, 2014.

Plate 5: Multiple unit 22000 class passing Sandymount stop, 2014.

Plate 6: Offices accessible from platform 2, Pearse Station, 2005.

Plate 7: Erne Terrace Rear from platform 2, Pearse Station, 2005.

Plate 8: Cumberland Street Bridge with one of the first trains out of Westland Row Station, coloured engraving by John Harris Jr, 1834.

Plate 9: Railway bridge to the reclaimed part of Grand Canal Basin, 2017.

Plate 10: Archway to Dodder bank and steps up to the railway bridge across the Dodder, 2010.

Plate 11: Booterstown Strand with the railway line in the middle of the photograph, 2015

Plate 12: The remaining lagoon in Booterstown Marsh at high tide, 2012.

Plate 13: View from Blackrock to Williamstown Martello tower, 1835. Coloured etching by J. Harris after a watercolour by Andrew Nichol.

Plate 14: Lord Cloncurry's towers and bridge. Painted by Andrew Nichol and engraved by John Harris.

Plate 15: Cutting through the rock, Lord Cloncurry's towers and footbridge in the background.

Plate 16: View from Seapoint towards Salthill.

Plate 17: Building on the site of former Seapoint Baths, view from the Seapoint Station footbridge, 2017.

Plate 18: Watercolour by A. Nichol, engraved by S.G. Hughes, *From the Martello Tower Bridge at Seapoint, looking towards Kingstown.*

Plate 19: Modern view from Seapoint Tower Bridge towards Dún Laoghaire, 2017.

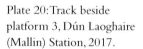

Plate 20: Track beside platform 3, Dún Laoghaire (Mallin) Station, 2017.

Signal box at Lansdowne Road level crossing, 2006.

Forrester and Company of Vauxhall Foundry, Liverpool, one of whose engines is depicted in the engraving of the first train leaving Westland Row and crossing Cumberland Street.

After this first year had passed, building and maintenance of engines and carriages moved to the south-east end of Grand Canal Dock, on a site that had previously held the Dock Distillery of Aeneas Coffey. The 1843 OS map shows the description 'Old Engine Ho.' in the area, but west of the railway and without a building. After some time, the plot where the first maintenance works had been near Lansdowne Road Station was used to build twelve cottages for railway workers.

The cottages are still there and much in demand, especially as most of them had modern extensions added to them that more than doubled the original living area. Car parking in this narrow cul-de-sac is not easy, though; the street is very narrow and there is hardly enough space at the end to turn a car.

In 1893, a siding was built from Lansdowne Road to Merrion Road, opposite the RDS. This side line ended where the AIB Banking Centre was

Railway Cottages, 2004.

later built. It transported horses to the RDS. At the time those horses crossed Merrion Road, any car traffic was halted and the cars simply had to wait until all the horses had been safely conducted across the road. During show times, for some time a shuttle service for passengers was run on that side line as well. The branch line was just 500m (*c*.1,600ft) long, but it saved horses and people a walk of around twice that length. It was closed for passenger traffic in 1943 and altogether in 1971.

At Serpentine Avenue, the next level crossing is reached. There had been a stop here in 1835, but only for two months. The reason for this is not clear as the RDS, which is quite near the level crossing of Serpentine Avenue, only moved into Ballsbridge in 1879. No trace of this short-lived station is left today, though in 1836 the almanac of Pettigrew & Oulton mentions a 'Railway Coffee House, John French, proprietor' on Serpentine Avenue. In 1837, the coffee house was still there, with the same name, but the proprietor

Path along the railway from Oaklands Park to Holyrood Park, 2008.

was listed as Charles Hayes and in 1838, it had again changed hands and was owned by Eliza Evans. From 1839 on, it was not mentioned any more.

Coming from Railway Cottages, one can walk beside the railway by crossing Serpentine Avenue and proceeding along Oaklands Park, until this street turns away from the rail line. A footpath, however, makes it possible to walk on, passing a structure that makes it (nearly) impossible even for a bicycle to pass through.

In summer, the entrance to this path is not always easy to find, depending on the growth of the bushes beside it and whether somebody has found time to cut them. The path is slightly sunken between the railway and a transformer station and ends on a street called Holyrood Park, which in itself leads, past Sandymount Station, to the level crossing at SandymountAvenue.

Like at so many other places along the railway and elsewhere, big walls without windows invite certain people to show their abilities as graffiti artists, as can also be seen when passing the Aviva Stadium on the DART.

In the 1930s, Sandymount Halt changed considerably. As John E. Mullee describes it:

> In 1937 this train stop had been adding features to make it a real railway station, and not just a halt. It got a station-master, a book stall, and – sure to be welcomed by passengers who got bored easily – more advertising.

J.E. Mullee also mentions that the article 'Sandymount Halt' in *The Irish Times* of 11 September 1937 reported that:

> Passengers taking the early train to Dublin one morning were surprised to find an iron footbridge over the tracks that certainly had not been there the night before. To add to this feat of moonlight construction, the station-proud residents of Sandymount considered their new bridge to be fit to take its place besides Sydney Harbour or San Francisco Bay.[35]

This footbridge must have been a delight for the children living nearby, who felt very adventurous standing on it while a train passed underneath as the bridge shook and the steam of the engine enveloped them. They probably occasionally also risked the gatekeeper's wrath when they stood on the gates while these were moved to close either the road or the railway.

The narrow footpath between the platform and the Holyrood 38 kV station, 2008.

Sandymount Station and Sandymount Avenue level crossing, 2012.

There are no level crossings with those old-fashioned gates on the line anymore, but the official Irish traffic sign announcing a level crossing with barriers still shows gates. When the signalling system of the railway was changed to electric signals, the traffic sign for a level crossing should also have been changed, showing warning lights and barriers. The newest sign shows the lights, but it shows neither barriers nor gates. Considering that the traffic sign was introduced to many level crossings long after steam engines had disappeared, the depiction of a train with a very old-fashioned steam engine is surprising, but somehow also endearing. Obviously the railway authorities wanted to be sure that trains would not be confused with trams.

With the coming of the DART, Sandymount Station was renewed, the old building removed and a new building erected. The gates disappeared and were replaced with barriers that move up and down instead of right and left.

The footbridge disappeared and an underpass was built to reach the other platform in case the barriers were down. Until some years ago, there was a second underpass as well for people who did not want to use the train, but just wanted to get to the other side of the level crossing. When automatic ticket-checking barriers were introduced in Sandymount, this underpass was blocked up.

Before the renewal of the Booterstown Station and the building of the Grand Canal Dock Station, the Sandymount Station building was the newest on the line and it won prizes for its architectural design.

The first improvement of the Sandymount stop occurred shortly after its second opening in 1860, but the stop was soon closed again in favour of Sydney Parade. Sandymount residents then demanded a footpath from the former Sandymount stop to Sydney Parade, but were not successful in their appeal. There is still no official path beside the railway between Sandymount

Awards won by Sandymount Station for its architectural design, 2008.

and Sydney Parade stations. Occasionally a train can be glimpsed when walking along Wilfield Road and looking up the lanes between the different blocks of houses on the south-west side of this street, which was developed between 1930 and 1945. Further on, one can get nearer the railway again, but only if one crosses private ground: the pitches of Monkstown FC and Pembroke CC.

From Sydney Parade Avenue, it is again possible to walk along the railway line for a stretch. This street and the whole area was named after Sidney Herbert, 1st Baron Herbert of Lea and second son of George Augustus Herbert, 11th Earl of Pembroke. From very early on, Dublin officials spelled the first name of Sidney Herbert with two 'y's for some reason. The 1843 OS map even named the area 'Sydney Parade' during the lifetime of the gentleman in question. Originally the Irish version of the station name, given above the English version, as was customary for street and station names, still kept the 'i':

Paráid Shidní
Sydney Parade

But soon afterwards English names kept their English form even in Irish-language signs and the sign now reads:

Sydney Parade
Paráid Sydney

Note that here the English name precedes the Irish name.

It is interesting that the station code for Sydney Parade is 'SIDNI', like in the older Irish version of the station name. The station code for Sandymount, SMONT, on the other hand, is an abbreviation of the English name of the station, not the Irish one, which is *Dumhach Thrá*.

Sydney Parade Station was in use longer than either Sandymount north of it or Merrion south of it, so it obviously served both villages and part of Ballsbridge as well. Some historical and literary facts about the station are documented in a bronze plaque in the shelter of the southbound platform in English and Irish. The English version of the bilingual text on the plaque reads:

Sydney Parade Station
Sydney Parade Station opened in 1835, soon after
the inauguration of the Dublin and Kingstown Railway,
becoming a busy intermediate station on the world's
first commuter railway line.
The basic 'halt' which first served the area was replaced by
a permanent structure in 1862, gradually acquiring shelters,
stone platforms, a brick building and a footbridge as befitted
one of the busiest stations on the line.
Sydney Parade is featured by James Joyce in DUBLINERS,
published in 1914, as the location for the death of Mrs. Emily
Sinico, in his short story, 'A Painful Case'.
Closed in 1960 during railway rationalisations of the period,
Sydney Parade re-opened in 1972 and generates over a
million journeys for the railway annually.

PRESENTED BY
AILSBURY PARK RESIDENTS ASSOCIATION
IN PARTNERSHIP WITH IARNRÓD ÉIREANN

Sydney Parade, like Lansdowne Road, has kept its signal box, which not only includes levers to change the signals, but also the big wheel to open and close the old gates (which are no longer there).

The introduction of those wheels must have been a godsend for the gatekeeper, who no longer had to go out into the open to move the big, heavy gates by hand, whatever the weather. Even looking in through the window, the impressive size of the wheel can be made out and gives an impression of the physical force needed to move the gates with the aid of the wheel and ropes.

Signal cabins like this one had been erected in 1925 at Westland Row, Grand Canal Street, Lansdowne Road, Serpentine Avenue, Sandymount, Sydney Parade, Merrion Gates, Blackrock, Salthill, Dunleary West Pier Crossing and one each at Dún Laoghaire North and South (plus an additional one on Carlisle Pier). Only Lansdowne Road and Sydney Parade are still in their original state.

From Sydney Parade to Merrion Gates, it is possible to walk along the railway again, firstly on the residential street Ailesbury Gardens and then on a footpath which leads to the car park of Merrion Hall. Before arriving at the car park, there is a footbridge across the railway.

Sydney Parade signal box, 2008.

Wheel to move gates inside Sydney Parade signal box, 2008.

Footbridge across the railway in Merrion, 2014.

On the Merrion footbridge across the railroad, 2014.

This is not the original footbridge, which was probably built at least partly of wood. Some of the pillars supporting the modern bridge are made of metal and seem to be older than the main part of the modern structure, which is built of stone and metal and is kept in good shape, as can be seen when crossing it.

This footbridge is rarely used today. It was possibly built mainly for people walking from the part of Merrion village east of the railway to the Merrion parish church of Our Lady, Queen of Peace, on Merrion Road. Nowadays, hardly anybody walks to Mass; most people drive, especially since the parish increased the size of the car park beside the church. This church has no window above the altar, probably because that it is the side of the church nearest the railway tracks.

Leaving this footbridge on the right, the path runs alongside the railway for a short stretch and ends at a little gate into the car park of the office

Merrion parish church on the other side of the railway, 2014.

Merrion Gates, *c.*1980. © Albert Bridge.

building that replaced the residential building called Merrion Hall. This name has been kept and is the only remainder of that building, which had been a private residence. The modern office building originally housed the head office of Córas Tráchtála.

Merrion Hall is only a few steps from the level crossing at Merrion Gates. Merrion Station was situated directly south of those gates, which, like other level crossings, had a signal hut. There are still small buildings there now, but old photographs indicate that the earlier signal box was like those that can still be seen on Lansdowne Road and Sydney Parade. The photograph also shows the old type of railway gates, as well as a material train beside what had been one of the platforms. By the looks of it, the engine is of the 071 class (see 'Rolling Stock'). The photograph was taken when the line was prepared for electrification.

The 'Water' Stretch

Nowadays, from Merrion Gates, there are two possible ways of following the railway southwards. Staying near the railway means some scrambling. The first part is easy. Even though the railway originally cut across a shallow bay from Merrion Gates, today enough sand has collected between the railway and the open sea that marram grass is growing there and sand dunes are starting to form (see Plate 11). Some small streams have to be crossed; therefore, it is advisable to wear wellingtons when walking this stretch.

Williamstown Martello tower is just visible on the right of the photograph (Plate 11), behind the railway line. As this part of the strand is not easily accessible, thousands of terns come every evening to roost here for the night. Seen from a distance, they make it look as if it is snowing, even in summer.

This stretch of sand was not there at all when the railway was built in 1834. In the beginning, the line went on a causeway across a flat bay of the sea. Considering the bad state of the Rock Road, which was very dusty in

A northbound train on its way from Booterstown to Merrion, 1835.

Former Merrion Station building, 2006.

dry weather and very muddy when wet, it is perhaps understandable that some people preferred to walk on the straight causeway on the bed of sand the tracks were laid into, instead of using the longer and much dirtier road. Especially during the early years, walking on the railway line seems to have been quite common, perhaps to some extent because people did not realise the danger of doing so. Later, only privileged people were allowed to do so and even that stopped from 1841, at least officially.

The easier way of following the railway today is to stay on the road, which is, in general, still where it was in the early 1830s, though it is now in better shape and is not as dirty any more, but it is often choked with cars, especially during rush hour. In the early nineteenth century, it still ran directly beside the sea. Just before the railway line left solid land and cut across the bay on the causeway, the trains passed (or stopped at) Merrion Station.

The village of Old Merrion was quite small when the railway line was built, but the station was probably erected for people who came there to bathe in the sea, as the 1843 map shows baths quite near the Merrion Gates. Some people also believe that the position of the station had something to do with the fact that one of the railway company directors lived nearby. The station was closed between 1860 and 1882. After the station was re-opened in 1882, a station building was erected in 1895, but the station was closed again in 1901. After that, it was opened again for a short time at the end of the 1920s and possibly during the first half of the 1930s. Today the platforms have disappeared and the former station building is used as a dwelling place.

Cutting across the bay meant that a lagoon was formed. This lagoon caused problems in the early years as it started to give off unpleasant smells. It took a number of years to solve the problem by connecting it with the sea through culverted passages under the railway. The 1843 OS map still notes that this area is 'Flooded at High Tides'. Part of it then began to silt up and finally became landfilled. This happened to the northernmost part of the rather big lagoon – the part that is still situated within the area of Dublin City (according to 1930s borders). This part now has a petrol station built on it, as well as a big office block, with its car park beside it. Across the border in County Dublin, there is still a tidal lagoon today and the causeway that had to be built to reach Booterstown Station in 1834 is still necessary.

The lagoon fills with seawater at high tide and becomes nearly completely dry at low tide. It is now a nature reserve consisting of the only remaining salt marsh and the only bird sanctuary in the southern part of Dublin Bay. It is managed by An Taisce. Birds on the lagoon can be watched from the northbound platform and birds on the strand from the southbound platform. Information panels show the different birds that visit the salt marsh.

RPSI train with locomotive no. 186 leaving Booterstown Station, 1968. © Michael Costello – IRRS collection; courtesy of Ciarán Cooney

The former station, however, has been taken down and a new station has been built with a footbridge across the tracks with stairs and lifts. This, as Plate 12 shows, is still beside the remains of the lagoon.

Some years ago, roadworks on the Rock Road resulted in a lot of material that had to be dumped. Instead of carting it off, it was decided to dump it into what remained of the lagoon to create two artificial islands. These islands have been welcomed by the birds that use the lagoon and occasionally DART users can observe a couple of grey herons and up to fifteen little egrets on these small islands, as well as other birds.

In the later twentieth century, the causeway to Booterstown Station was widened and a car park was built on its north-western side. The south-eastern part of what was a lagoon is nearly completely infilled now and has been turned into a little park with a good playground for children. Only a small, tidal stream is left beside the railway on the land side. This is connected with the remaining lagoon on the other side of the causeway, with a centuries-old outlet to the sea opposite Willow Terrace at the northern end of the grounds of Blackrock College.

It might be possible to walk along the railway between Booterstown and Merrion, on the sea side, but only at low tide and preferably in wellingtons. At high tide, the sea reaches right up to the embankment for the railway.

New station building in Booterstown, 2012.

View from Booterstown Station northwards towards Merrion, 2014.

Between Booterstown Station and the Williamstown Martello tower, the 1843 OS map shows two culverts or tunnels under the railway in the area that still flooded at high tide. These led to tidal streams runninh through the sandy strand into the sea. The western tunnel is still there today and allows seawater in and out of the Booterstown Marsh lagoon.

The railway barely touched solid land at Williamstown Martello tower in 1834, where the short-lived Williamstown Station had been installed. This station was used by more people than one might expect, given the small size of the village of Williamstown. This was because the Dublin & Kingstown Railway Company had built sea baths west of the station, at the eastern end of the lagoon. The railway company sold combined tickets for the travel to and the use of the baths. On the 1843 OS map, 'Baths' are mentioned west of the Martello tower and south of the railway, whereas between the railway and the sea a 'Bath Ho.' is mentioned. This was obviously meant for people who preferred the fresher waters of the sea to the calmer waters in the lagoon. East and west of the Martello tower, the area is still described on this old map as 'Flooded at High Tides'. According to the same map, people who had used the bathhouse or bathed in the sea would have to cross the railway to reach the northbound platform without any special provision. The 1912 OS map also mentions a bathing place, though not a bathhouse. At that time, there was a footbridge across the railway. Today there is still a footbridge in the same location.

Compared with Sandymount Martello tower, the tower at Williamstown looks rather low. When it was built, it was the same height as all of the other Martello towers. At that time, it would have been surrounded by seawater at high tide. It was not until the area was filled in to form part of what later became Blackrock Park that the tower was to be continuously on dry land and of course infilling raised the ground level. That part of the tower which is visible today is actually the first floor as the ground floor today is buried underground.[36]

The next stretch cut through the bay again, but this causeway was not as long as the one from Merrion to Booterstown had been. Still, in old

Williamstown Martello tower and footbridge, 2017.

pictures (see Plate 13), the stretch looks long enough and one wonders if trains would have been able to cross the causeway in high winds as the waves must surely have splashed against it.

The lagoon in the left of the picture (Plate 13) was filled in rather quickly. In 1873, Blackrock Park was built on this spot, with a bandstand, a pool with a little island where ducks and other birds nest and some walks (other than the path between Booterstown and Blackrock stations). The dark-coloured rock, however, which had given rise to the name 'Black Rock', disappeared under the park when it was built.

The 1843 map shows three culverts or tunnels on the stretch between Williamstown Tower and Blackrock Station, but curiously enough only two of them are shown as water outlets to the sea, even at low water mark. The first of those has disappeared on the 1912 OS map, which shows the second one with a semicircle touching the railway line on its south-western side and described as 'Sand'. The culvert and semicircle are still there today, but inside the semicircle is an ESB building. The third of the three 1843 culverts has a similar structure in the 1912 map, without the inscription 'Sand'. Today, this is the northern end of the stream coming in from Blackrock and flowing north-west along the railway until it enters the sea through the tunnel under the railway at that spot. The pool in Blackrock Park might be connected with this stream, as a thin line on the 1912 map indicates.

Blackrock Park still has its bandstand, but it also has a playground, flower beds, bushes and trees and it has not only been well accepted by the Blackrock people, but also by the birds of the area. For that reason, some trees have been left standing, even though they have been dead for quite some time.

Just before Blackrock Station, a rocky outcrop reaches nearly to the edge of the sea, with the footpath squeezed in between a low cliff and the railway, which touches land again at that spot. Blackrock Station is one of the stations designed by the architect John Skipton Mulvany. According to the *Dictionary of Irish Architects*, it was built in 1841.[37] The land-side façade is still as Mulvany had envisioned it.

Blackrock was the second station, after Williamstown, with a big sea bath run by the railway company. This was built as early as 1839. In the beginning, there was just a walled pool built into the sea at Blackrock Station. It could be overlooked from Idrone Terrace.

Later, at the sea end of the pool, a diving tower was built. This bath was a popular spot in the summer and the tower indicates that the water at that end

Herring gulls and (sleeping) grey heron in a dead tree in Blackrock Park, 2016.

Blackrock Station, façade of 1841 by J.S. Mulvany, 2017.

Idrone Terrace, Blackrock, with the Blackrock Bath, *c.*1910; from an old postcard.

Blackrock Bath beside Blackrock Station, *c.*1930; from an old postcard.

Remains of Blackrock Bath from the footbridge on Blackrock Station, 2016.

of the bath must have been rather deep. This stretch of the coast is quite rocky and it must have been easy to dig into the rocks and keep a deep pool there.

The bath is no longer in use and in the past few years even the diving tower has been taken down. Some structures are still there, though, and from the modern footbridge across the railway line at that station, the fury of the sea thrashing against the remains of that bath can sometimes be seen, with Howth in the background.

East of those former baths, the 1843 OS map shows a 'Gentlemens' [*sic*] Bathing Place' and a bit further east a 'Ladies [*sic*] Bathing Place'. Both bathing places were separated by a rocky outcrop that descended into the sea between them. The street leading to those baths is still called 'Bath Place' today.

The border of the 'Co. of the City and the 'Parliamentary Border' also reached the sea between these two bathing places in 1843. Until the Municipal Corporation Reform (Ireland) Act in 1840, the area administered by the City of Dublin included Blackrock Station – but not Blackrock Village! In 1840, the area of Dublin City was much reduced and only included the area between the canals. Blackrock, station and village, became part of the Barony of Rathdown in the County of Dublin. Blackrock Township was founded in 1863 and took over some of the administrative responsibility that until then had rested with the Grand Jury of the County.

The End Bit

A short distance after those bathing places, the stretch of the railway line towards Dún Laoghaire (then still called Kingstown) became the most expensive part to build. As well as rocks that the railway engineers had to cut through, there were influential landowners who objected to having a railway built between their residence on the cliff and their bathing place below. In other cases, the railway company attained the right of compulsory purchase, but in the case of two landowners it did not get that right and had to use other means to convince the owners of the land to agree to the building of a railway across their property. The original plan shown to parliament included a tunnel under the grounds of Lord Cloncurry and the Rev. Sir Harvey Lees. This tunnel was supposed to be 500 yards (460 metres) long and would have to be constructed through solid rock. Obviously it was decided that this would be too costly. The landowners probably would have objected that building this tunnel was even more disruptive for them and consequently the line was moved further north, which meant that half its length on that stretch would be on causeways across small bays and inlets. Even this line, which was ultimately what was built, cut through bits of land owned by the gentlemen mentioned above. Negotiations started and took their time. The idea of a tunnel was not abandoned.

Lord Cloncurry's Demands

The objections of one of the owners in question, the Rev. Sir Harvey Lees of Blackrock House, were finally overcome when he was paid a sum of £7,500 and it was decided that a wooden bridge would be built from his land across the railway to the seashore as compensation for the

Maretimo, Blackrock.

inconvenience. Slightly further west of him, Valentine Lawless, 2nd Baron Cloncurry was not as easy to convince. His main estates were situated in Lyons in Co. Kildare, but he also owned a house in Blackrock, which was called Maretimo.

The house is on the 1912 map, but it was demolished in 1970. Lord Cloncurry originally insisted on what he called a 'tunnel'. This was not the 500-yard-long tunnel in the plans for parliament, but a shorter version. Drawings of this intended tunnel exist and show that by 'tunnel', he might have meant a long building through which the train would have to travel, out of sight of Lord Cloncurry, his family and guests. The trains would go behind the pillars, at least partly out of view of the house. The steam, however, would come out from between the pillars. Another view shows this 'tunnel' as seen from the air.[38]

One detail in this engraving is interesting, as it is incorrect but also appears in the depiction of the structure that was finally built and will be discussed later. The drawings shown above were not only produced in the *Penny Journal*, of which P. Dixon Hardy was the publisher, but also

'Tunnel' as it would have been seen from Maretimo; as shown in the *Penny Journal*, 1834.

Aerial view of Lord Cloncurry's planned tunnel; as shown in the *Penny Journal*, 1834.

in *The Dublin and Kingstown Railway,* by the same publisher, P. Dixon Hardy, printed in Dublin in 1834. These views were published before the railway was finished and Dixon explained that some details might have been changed during the building of the railway line. Lord Cloncurry got the railway company to provide him with towers, piers, bridges and a bathing place, including a mock temple 'in the best Italian style', on top of gracefully agreeing to accept £3,000 as compensation. The tunnel as shown in Dixon's illustration was never built, though, and only one set of towers with a footbridge was erected.

The construction of the railway was important enough to produce many reports, including illustrations, before, during and after the time when it was being built. The stretch from Blackrock to Salthill via Seapoint, however, with its cliffs, bridges and stretches cut through rock, aroused the interest of a number of artists. The most famous of them is Andrew Nichol, who created a series of watercolours which were then used by others for engravings after Nichol's pictures. The best-known engravers were John Harris, S.G. Hughes and R. Clayton. Some engravers worked from the same watercolour, but it is astonishing in how many details those engravings differ.

Plate 14 clearly shows a grave mistake, the same mistake that is shown in the engraving of the plan of the 'tunnel' mentioned above: the trains are depicted on the wrong track! Even before the railway was opened to the public, the Dublin & Kingstown Railway Company had introduced 'Rules and regulations to be observed by Engine Men, Guards, Policemen, & other Servants of the Company'. The first regulation points out a very important rule:

> The Locomotive Engine shall in every case pass along the Left Hand line of rails looking in the direction the Train is travelling, that is, when going to Kingstown on the North line & when going to Dublin on the South line.[39]

Both on the engraving of the planned 'tunnel' and on J. Harris' engraving of Lord Cloncurry's towers and footbridge, the train passes on the right and not the left side of the line.

On another engraving, the trains use the right tracks, but there are a number of other differences compared with the J. Harris engraving.

On Clayton's engraving, the trains use the proper tracks and the carriages look a bit more like how they were at that time. Harris' engraving (Plate 14) has the train on the wrong track and the carriages too high. Further

Lord Cloncurry's towers and bridge. Engraved by Robert Clayton after the painting by Andrew Nichol.

differences between the two engravings are: the width of the windows compared with the width of the towers; the proportions of the three steps on the tower roofs; the urn/sphere on top of the towers and the end of the sea wall with respect to the tower.

In addition, compared with the engraving of the planned 'tunnel', neither of the two engravings of the towers that were actually built shows the footbridge from Lord Cloncurry's land to the land-side tower, which is shown in the plan of the 'tunnel' and which still exists today.

The modern photograph shows the sea wall swinging around the seaward tower and not touching it at all, though it is depicted as touching it in the old engravings.

When walking on the rough path north of the rail tracks, in some places the old granite sleepers appear, mostly the short version of the sleepers, but there is occasionally also a long one. Some still bear the holes where the rails were fixed onto the sleepers. However, they are not in their original place. It was soon found that the combination of stone sleepers with the weight and movement of the locomotives damaged the rails in a very short time. Stone

Lord Cloncurry's towers and bridge, 2017.

sleepers were quickly replaced by wooden sleepers. The intention had been to sell the old granite sleepers, but it was difficult to find any takers. Most of the granite sleepers were then re-used by the railway company to build a promenade between the railway line and the sea. It is still possible to walk on a short stretch of this promenade between Blackrock Station and Lord Cloncurry's towers, but it looks as if it will be completely overgrown in the near future.

Some of the sleepers still contain at least one of the iron bolts that were used to fix the rail onto the sleeper.

Lord Cloncurry did get a kind of tunnel at the eastern end of the Maretimo grounds. This 'tunnel' was more a wide, natural bridge to his private bathing place and pier, which was clad with stonework on both sides. Later, a small private boat harbour was built on the part of his land north of the railway as well. Again the engraving by J. Harris after the picture by A. Nichol is not quite right, as Plate 15 shows.

The full title of Nichol's picture (Plate 15) is *Dublin and Kingstown Railway. The Tunnel from the Excavation, looking towards Dublin.* It was more likely the

Promenade built with short and long granite sleepers, with holes to fix the rails, 2017.

Granite sleeper with iron bolt, 2017.

engraver than the painter who made the mistake with the lines for the track on the left of the picture, as there are four lines instead of two for this track. Those lines converge in the distance in front of a train. This train is also not depicted correctly, as it obviously goes in the same direction as the train in the foreground, even though it uses the other track. And no old railway carriage had windows facing the locomotive. Health and safety was less important in those times than it is now. Apart from people watching the train from the bridge, the picture shows two persons standing at the foot on the bridge near the tracks. They could only have got there by walking on the tracks.

The tunnel is still there and anybody who ever took the DART between Blackrock and Seapoint will know that, though it is not a long tunnel at all, it is longer than it seems in the picture. Old plans for the line give the tunnel's length as 70ft (21 metres); it is 9 metres (30ft) wide and 7.3 metres (24ft) high. The sides of the cutting are secured by walls today and so are the two ends of the 'tunnel', as is shown in the engraving. Considering the width of the cutting, it would definitely not be advisable to stand at the foot of the bridge beside the tracks nowadays.

Lord Cloncurry's 'tunnel', still with the footbridge in the background, 2017.

Access to Seapoint DART Station, 2017.

The Rev. Sir Harvey Lees was paid two and a half times as much money as Lord Cloncurry for giving up more or less the same amount of land, but he only got a wooden bridge to cross the railway and neither a private bathing place nor a private pier, as Lord Cloncurry did. Also, Sir Harvey's bridge was far less elaborate than Lord Cloncurry's.

Seapoint

On a rather short stretch to the east of the 'Wooden Br.' on Sir Harvey Lees' land, the 1843 OS map shows two more wooden bridges. Between them, on a piece of land with cliffs down to the railway, the same map shows two buildings. One of them is named 'Seapoint College' and the first wooden bridge goes from this college to a boat slip on the other side of the railway. This footbridge is still there, though it is not a wooden bridge any more. It starts at the back of the houses of Ardenza Terrace and is not open to the general public.

Finding Seapoint DART Station from the public road (Seapoint Avenue) is not easy, as the station is lower than Seapoint Avenue and the access path is very narrow and leads off Seapoint Avenue between the eastern turn into Ardenza Terrace and the entrance to house no. 34. It just looks like the entrance to another private building.

There are different versions of the history of the Seapoint halt/Seapoint Station. One version says it was opened in 1837 and stayed open until 1960, before re-opening for the DART. However, the 1843 OS map that names all stations on the then Dublin & Kingstown Railway does not show a station or a halt at Seapoint. Other sources say that the station was opened in 1862, was originally called 'Monkstown and Seapoint', got its station building in 1863 and has been remodelled since. In parts, it still shows its Victorian provenance. The fact that the 1834 map does not show it makes it likely that the second version is true. The misunderstanding might come from the original name 'Monkstown and Seapoint' as the station known as 'Salthill and Monkstown' definitely was opened in 1837 and stayed open until 1960, re-opening for the DART in 1984.

For the station building, some stabling had to be taken down and as compensation a new building was erected, with some interesting round windows and a balustrade on part of its top. The building is not used as a stable any more and the circular windows in the wall facing the platform

Part of Seapoint DART Station building, 2017.

are rather puzzling for many DART users, some of whom erroneously think that the building is a former engine shed.

At the eastern end of Ardenza Terrace, which is shown on the 1912 OS map, the 1843 map shows 'Seapoint Ho.' The abbreviation 'Ho.' usually stands for 'House'. As on the same map Salthill Hotel is named as 'Salt Hill Ho.', the building could have been Seapoint Hotel instead of Seapoint House. Another of Andrew Nichol's watercolours, again engraved by J. Harris, shows a view towards Salthill from a footbridge near Seapoint Hotel.

This engraving, entitled *Dublin and Kingstown Railway, From the Foot Bridge at Sea Point Hotel, looking towards Salt Hill. Kingstown Harbor [sic] in the distance*, is shown on Plate 16. According to the 1843 OS map, there were two footbridges in the area, one near Seapoint Hotel, the second crossing the railway tracks at Seapoint halt. It is not clear which of the two footbridges is meant. If it was the one at the station, the interestingly shaped building roughly in the middle of the picture would be a building belonging to Seapoint Baths. In that case, the second footbridge, shortly east (behind) this building should be shown. There is no other footbridge depicted, which might lead one to believe that the picture would have to have been taken from the wooden bridge after Seapoint Hotel, the one that leads from Seapoint Avenue to the baths. But then there should not be any building between this bridge and the Seapoint Martello Tower Bridge, which can be seen in the far background. These are the facts. From the viewpoint of an artist, the situation could be different. The building on the left is needed to counteract the steep hill on the right or else the picture might look lopsided. On the other hand, a footbridge directly after the building would interfere with the composition of the picture by producing a straight line crossing the straight lines of the tracks. Thus they would disturb the balance the artist might have had in mind.

Considering that the second footbridge has been left out, the building in the picture is part of what is shown on both the 1843 and the 1912 OS map, in 1843 called 'Bath' and in 1912 'Seapoint Baths' south of the railway and 'Ladies Bathing Place' north of it. On the 1912 map, it is referred to as what it still is today: the house at the western end of the cul-de-sac with the name 'Brighton Vale'. It has retained its unusual shape, as Plate 17 shows.

For a short stretch to the east of Seapoint Station, the railway line runs in another cutting that had a road on its south side (now Seapoint Avenue) and bare rock on the north side, as the 1843 map shows. In 1846, a terrace of houses was built in a cul-de-sac reaching westward from the Martello Tower Bridge. It was built by John Skipton Mulvany, who for some time seems to have lived in one of those houses himself.[40] This is the only residential street between the railway and the sea on the stretch from Merrion Gates to the West Pier of Dún Laoghaire Harbour. When seen from Seapoint Avenue, it is only the overhead wires that give away the railway line in the cutting.

The only artificial road bridge over the railway line between Dublin and the original terminus at Salthill is the bridge that was built to get provisions to Seapoint Martello tower, described on the 1843 map as 'Tower Br'. This bridge, which was also called 'Ordnance Bridge', had to be sturdy as the material carried across included cannons, cannonballs and other ammunition. Today, the bridge is also used to give car access to the houses on Brighton Vale.

The Seapoint Martello tower, officially called Martello Tower Dublin South No. 14, was restored during the last years of the twentieth century. After the restoration, it was used as the headquarters of the Genealogical Society, which, however, found after some time that it was too damp,

Backs of the houses on Brighton Vale, seen across the railway line from Seapoint Avenue, 2017.

Seapoint Martello tower and Martello Tower Bridge, 2017.

especially for an archive. Since 2011, it has been a small museum, which can be visited.[41] In 2012, its cannon was returned to its roof.

It is also interesting to note that even though the Dublin & Kingstown Railway company built and ran a number of baths along the railway line, in the nineteenth century, there was no bathing place at the Seapoint Martello tower. Seapoint Baths were much nearer Seapoint Station at the western end of what now is Brighton Vale and near the eastern end of the platforms of Seapoint Station. A further bathing place is shown both on the 1843 and the 1912 OS map at the middle of the little bay. Nowadays, the bathing place at Seapoint Tower is one of the biggest and best-known bathing places in Dublin Bay. It has been a Blue Flag strand for many years. At the time of writing, in 2017, it was the only one on the coast of Co. Dublin south of the Liffey.

The little cul-de-sac Brighton Vale was fully built up in 1912. It is reached on the western end by a footbridge across the railway from Seapoint Avenue and via the Ordnance Bridge on the eastern end. The sea can be seen from the street, but not the railway, as this runs in a cutting and the row of houses blocks the view anyway.

Apart from scrambling over rocks or, depending on the tide, swimming around those rocks from the former Seapoint Baths, the sea can be reached from Seapoint Avenue using a footbridge across the railway. This bridge is shown as a wooden bridge in 1843. In 1912, Seapoint Avenue did not exist yet, but the bridge is shown as a pedestrian continuation of Albany Avenue. The view of the coast and the railway is depicted in another watercolour by Andrew Nichol, entitled *From the Martello Tower Bridge at Seapoint, looking towards Kingstown*; this time the engraver was S.G. Hughes. His engraving shows five rails for two tracks (Plate 18).

Plate 18 shows a view of the cove which in the 1843 map was depicted as a sandy stretch with some rocks, including 'Seal Rock', and in the 1912 map it had a 'Bathing Place' to which the aforementioned footbridge led. On that map, Seal Rock is shown beyond the sandy area, in the sea.

Seapoint Avenue, as a road continuing from Monkstown to Dún Laoghaire along the coast, is relatively modern. In 1843, it turned south into Seafield Avenue, with just a short cul-de-sac towards two houses east of Seafield Avenue. From there, a narrow lane or path continued to the end of Brighton Terrace, a short cul-de-sac turning westwards from the northern end of Brighton Avenue. The 1912 map shows the same situation with the additional information that the last house on Seapoint Avenue (the cul-de-sac part) was called 'Azar' and the path continuing eastwards from there was called 'Azar Passage'. Part of that path still seems to be there, leading down the steep hill. The modern Seapoint Avenue (N31) runs straight to Albany Avenue. A house called 'Seafield Cottage' on the 1912 map had to be taken down to build the road. The footbridge across the railway from east of Seafield Cottage to the rocks/bathing place that is shown on the 1843 map is there still, though most likely in a modernised form. Nichol's watercolour does not show this footbridge; instead, it depicts a small kind of factory or, at least, a small building with a tall chimney emitting blackish smoke. Neither the 1843 nor the 1912 map shows anything that might correlate with this building.

Another stretch of road that was not there in 1912 was the short stretch between Brighton Terrace and Clifton Terrace. Both the 1843 and the 1912 maps show a narrow lane that goes past a house, which, in 1843, is named as 'Brighton Villa'. The house is still there, now, as then, a short distance south of the road. Plate 19 gives the modern view from Seapoint Avenue, which shows that the bay is much wider than could be expected from Nichol's watercolour. Monkstown church can just barely be made out on the far right of the photograph and Dún Laoghaire Harbour is much farther away than Nichol makes his viewer believe. On top of that, the modern picture shows many more buildings between Monkstown and Dún Laoghaire.

Salthill and its Hotel

Nichol's view of the railway and the coast at Monkstown shows the distinctive Monkstown church on the right and Salthill House in the centre. Between both buildings, the land near the coast seems to dip down from Monkstown village and rise up again to Salthill House. This building was owned by the railway company. It was situated above the Salthill and Monkstown Station. John Skipton Mulvany was asked to provide plans for additions to the building. The plans were finished in 1836, but only executed in 1843.[42] This building is shown on the 1843 map as 'Salt Hill Ho.', which was opened as Salthill Hotel in December 1834, at the same time as the railway line. Its footprint is different from that of the Salt Hill Hotel shown on the 1912 map and the footbridge from the hotel to the bathing place does not seem to be there yet, though a bathing place is shown on the 1843 map on the other side of the railway from the hotel. The building was extended again in the 1860s.

Salthill Hotel and its footbridge to beach and railway station, *c.*1870; from an old postcard.

This view from the sea seems to be idealised, as other views indicate that the seashore there was part sandy, part rocky, but in no case suitable for sailing as near the waterline as the postcard seems to indicate. As far as the footbridge is concerned, an earlier view from the same viewing point shows the first pillar supporting the footbridge as square and the second as round, with the stairs winding around it. The square pillar has disappeared but the circular pillar still exists; however, it is so near the train tracks, from which it is separated by a tall fence, that it is nearly unbelievable that in former times a spiral staircase wound around it without getting in the way of the trains.

During the first year of the railway, this station was the terminus, but it was not as grandly designed and built as the later Kingstown (Dún Laoghaire) Station. The reason for this was that the railway company knew already that they would have to build an extension to the railway, as discussed below.

The platform on the sea side of the station is separated from the footpath beside it by a fence, but the shelter at the end of the platform can obviously

Pillar that held the spiral staircase from the Salthill Hotel footbridge, 2017.

Salthill Station with Salthill Hotel in the background, *c.*1900, from an old postcard.

be used both from the path and the platform. In the background (centre left of the photograph), a train is approaching the station on its way to Dublin. The hotel was probably the main reason why this station was kept open when the line was extended from Salthill to Kingstown, which is hardly more than half a mile (less than 700 metres) away. Guests of the hotel could reach the station, as well as the beach, from the hotel on foot, using the footbridge that had been built for their convenience.

Salthill Hotel burnt down in 1970 and was demolished in 1972. A big block of apartments was built on the site.

The modern photograph shows that there is indeed a dip in the land behind the railway. This is where the car park has been built for the Salthill and Monkstown Station of modern times.

There were never grand buildings at this first terminus of the line at Salthill. When the line was planned, the docking of the mail boats had been planned for the west pier and for this Salthill would have been the right place for a terminus. While the line was being built, the harbour commissioners changed their mind and decided to have the mail boats come in much nearer

Apartment block on the site of the former Salthill Hotel, 2017.

the east pier. This meant that the railway line would need to be extended. This was already known in 1834, so that Salthill was regarded as a provisional terminus, even though Kingstown was only reached in 1837. To get there, the Kingstown Martello tower had to be demolished, for which permission had to be sought, a process that took quite some time. Also, some of the old Dunleary Harbour was cut off from the sea, which necessitated consultations with the Harbour board. This part was later reclaimed and gasworks were built on the new land. The Martello tower and the southernmost part of old Dunleary harbour would have been on the south of the railway tracks. The coastguard station, further east and on the north of the tracks, was built in 1863.[43]

The last stretch the railway line ran parallel to the 'truck railway', better known as 'The Metals', the truck line on which granite blocks to build the west pier were brought from Dalkey Quarry. The tracks are no longer there, but on a short stretch one can clearly see where this truck railway had been. It was removed after the work for which it was there – building the west pier – had finished.

There were two bridges at this spot. The first was built in 1837, with one single, elliptical arch, but in 1854 the roads were lowered, which meant that a new bridge had to be built. This new bridge had three arches, two for the railway and a third for the former truck way. This might have been the bridge which had so little headroom that the company had to forbid passengers from riding on the roofs of the carriages, as they had done at least occasionally until then. With the advent of electrification, the surviving bridge had to be changed again, but it still seems to be rather low.

It is interesting to observe that this new bridge still has room to accommodate the former horse-drawn trucks, even though those tracks, which had seen extensive use while Kingstown (Dún Laoghaire) Harbour was being built, have not been used for many decades.

It is usual to speak of Kingstown (Dún Laoghaire) as a terminus. Strictly speaking, it was not one terminus, but two. A detailed inspection of the Dún Laoghaire (Mallin) Station of today allows one to differentiate between the former terminus of the D&KR and the former terminus of the Atmospheric Railway from Dalkey to Kingstown (Dún Laoghaire). Of the two tracks that led into the D&KR terminus, only one is still left (shown on Plate 20). This track is today used for trains starting or terminating in Dún Laoghaire. Part of the space for the other track is tarmacadamed now and used for cars.

Bridge accessing Harbour Road and Accommodation Road, 2017.

DART arrival at Dún Laoghaire (Mallin) Station, 2017.

What is now the track and platform part of the DART station used to be the terminus of the Atmospheric Railway and it was only when the extension to Dalkey and Bray replaced the Atmospheric Railway that the two lines were connected. This also resulted in a change of the gauge in the mid-1850s from the original standard gauge (1,435mm/4ft 8½in) of the D&KR to the Irish gauge (1,600mm/5ft 3in) still in use today.

The last stretch of the Atmospheric Railway ran under Queen's Road and arrived at the terminus literally 'out of the darkness'.

As the line was only used by one train, only one track was necessary. Today, the line runs for a much longer stretch under Queen's Road, but it still arrives out of the darkness.

Actually even after the extension towards Bray was finished and working, the stretch southwards out of Dún Laoghaire Station as far as the branch-off towards Carlisle Pier was a single track for a long time. Short as this single track stretch was, it created an awkward bottleneck, which was signal-controlled. The situation was only remedied by CIÉ in 1957.

Walls of the former terminus hall of the D&KR (on left of DART train), 2017.

Other changes have also been made to the Dún Laoghaire (Mallin) Station. The roof over the railway hall of the former terminus has disappeared, though the walls are still there and in some places show where windows might once have been.

The former terminus of the Atmospheric Railway used to have a roof over its platform in earlier times. This has disappeared now, but traces can still be seen beside what was possibly part of the station building of the Atmospheric Railway.

Another photograph makes it clear that the two stations were separate buildings, side by side, in different styles and without any connection with each other. Despite the fact that both the line from Kingstown to Dublin and the Atmospheric line from Kingstown to Dalkey were run by the D&KR company, separate tickets were necessary, even for passengers who wanted to go from Dublin to Dalkey. The train times were co-ordinated, in principle, so that passengers did not need to wait at Kingstown Station. It did happen, however, that a train would arrive late and passengers would not have

Traces of former platform roof, Dún Laoghaire (Mallin) Station, 2017.

Station buildings of Dún Laoghaire (Mallin) Station, 2017.

enough time to buy a ticket for the other train. For regulars, the problem was at least partly solved by the availability of ticket books containing ten tickets, so they could change directly from one train to the other. They still had to change platforms, though.

Even though the building that used to be the terminus building for the D&KR, which has been a restaurant for many years, should be the end of the line, one concession has to be made concerning the length of the line. The Dublin & Kingstown Railway was built to bring the Royal Mail and passengers of the mail boats from the harbour in Kingstown (Dún Laoghaire) to Dublin. When the number of passengers increased, it was felt that it was not appropriate that so many people should have to walk the 350 metres or so from the train terminal to the ferry terminal. Especially in inclement weather, this would not have been pleasant at all and managing luggage was not easy either. Therefore, a siding was built leading out of the railway terminus and onto Carlisle Pier, where the mail boats docked. The tracks of that siding have disappeared, but the opening from the tunnel

Site of the siding towards Carlisle Pier, 2017.

under Queen's Road still can be seen just east of the Royal St George Yacht Club.

Carlisle Pier is still there, but it has been completely cleared of buildings. The railway station was closed in 1980. The train platforms and tracks and the docking terminal, which was closed two years later in 1982, are only memories and the future of Carlisle Pier is uncertain. (The Genealogical Society of Ireland gives 'Carlisle Pier' as its address, but their headquarters is opposite, rather than on, the pier, under the monument of George IV.)

Memories of Railway Passengers

There are some anecdotes from the early years of the D&K Railway, but no written or orally reported memories seem to exist from the first half-century of this railway line. An early memory from the end of the nineteenth century was recorded by William Richard Le Fanu in his memoirs, as mentioned in the section about rolling stock.

For the first half of the twentieth century, the Vincentian Fr Tom Davitt (grandson of Michael Davitt) wrote in the journal of the IRRS about his memories of the time between 1934 and 1946, when his family lived in Sydney Parade, near the station. Despite the span of seventy-odd years between the events he describes and the time when he wrote them down, his reported observations are exact, in as far as they can be checked today.

According to Fr Davitt, Sydney Parade was a station, whereas Sandymount and Booterstown were only halts. As a station, it had a station master who lived opposite the station, with the front door and windows of his house facing the railway line instead of the street. As a boy, Fr Davitt, his elder brother and their friends seem to have been in and out of the signal box, which he remembers as only being closed on Sundays during the 'Emergency', as there were no trains then. During the week, there were even trains during the night. Most of the station's amenities were on the 'Up' platform (now called the 'northbound' platform). There was a general waiting room, but also a ladies' waiting room, each with a fireplace, though Fr Davitt never saw a fire lit in them. There were toilets: the gents' were accessed from the platform and the ladies from the ladies' waiting room. There were vending machines for sweets and cigarettes and even a weighing machine. From the mid-1930s, he remembers a short-lived kiosk at the street end of the 'Up' platform and after that a little shop on the street side of the 'Down' ('southbound') platform. Accidents occurred, but rarely:

On one occasion, which I cannot date, the front wheels of the bogie of either a 4-6-0T or a 4-4-2T became derailed at the Sandymount end of the Sydney Parade station platform. I do not know how this happened, or how they re-railed it, but I have a distinct memory of seeing it.[44]

Trains had other uses for the young Tom Davitt and were not merely objects to be inspected or means of travel. They helped to remember the time. During the long bright summer evenings, the sound of the goods train going towards Wexford made him realise that it was ten o'clock and therefore time to go home.

Up until 1960, most of the stations between Westland Row and Dún Laoghaire that are now DART stations were in service (with the exception of Sandymount, which was only re-opened in 1928, and the Grand Canal Dock Station, which only was built in 2001). This meant that in those years trains were used to get to town as they were faster than trams (which stopped going in the 1940s) and buses.

John Eugene Mullee, who grew up a four-minute walk from Sandymount Station, took the train to go to the Christian Brothers' school on Westland Row. His description of his experiences is worth quoting at length:

Until I was about ten years of age, I used to take a steam train to school every day. I never got tired of watching the huge pistons and levers groan and strain as they coaxed the iron monster out of its inertia. It was like trying to move a big old dog who was determined to stay lying down. First, steam hissed and puffed from jets and nozzles on the engine's belly; then the giant wheels started to turn – slowly and reluctantly – inching the whole train forward; the first thunderous puff from the chimney shot a blast of steam and smoke that billowed up under the glass roof of Westland Row Railway Station; then the huge chain links tying the rail cars together started to clink one by one as they took up the load. That first laboured puff was followed slowly by another, slightly less strained, then another and another, until they began to come quicker and easier. If you stood real close to the engine (as I always did) you could feel the thrust of energy within your body.

But once in a while a string of railroad cars refused to yield to the brute force of steam. Something had to give: the wheels lost their grip on the rails, and all hell broke loose. A thunderous explosion shook the very guts in your belly and vibrated your rib cage (making you suddenly aware that you had one).

The wheels now spun free in a paroxysm of epileptic convulsion, while the train stood still. Pistons, levers and rods jerked in and out rapidly, hissing and blowing hot steam. The chimney belched out black smoke in five or six rapid-fire shots. All through this you could smell the heated grease and oil from the pistons, and you even had the sensation of tasting it. Now the steam engine had got to all five of your senses.

Maybe even a certain sixth sense.

Eventually the steam would win, of course, and the carriages would crawl forward obediently. As soon as the engine cleared the cavernous roof of the railway station, there was a sudden quieting. Only the jerking and squealing of steel scraping against steel remained, and soon this was gone, too. There was what passed for quiet in the station, while the smoke and steam trapped under the big glass roof found its way to the two gable ends of the station, and escaped into the indifferent Dublin sky.

Then the sound of human voices could be heard again, at least until the next train thundered in.[45]

Concerning different classes in the carriages, the above chapter about rolling stock mentions that the Drumm trains had first and third class, but no second class. J.E. Mullee remembers that this was also the case on the steam trains that he was used to as a child. He wonders whether the decision not to have a 'second-class passenger' was made because it might smack too much of a 'second-class person'. The heating system in the trains was obviously the same for both classes, as Mullee recalls:

> The entire train was heated liberally by steam radiators. Judging by how hot it was in our compartment, I doubt if we had any less steam than the First Class passengers. Occasionally, a small wisp of steam would escape from the radiator under your seat and rise up past your legs and arms. Steam has a smell, and this was quite a pleasant experience, a bit weird and unusual but strangely agreeable.[46]

In Germany, at least some railway companies went another way when they reduced the number of ticket classes from three to two: they eliminated first class! For years, in the 1950s and 1960s, there was only second class and third class, until finally second class was renamed first class and what had been third class was renamed second class. There was no change to the service or the level of comfort; actually, nothing changed except the numbers on the doors of the railway cars.

Fr Davitt seems to have been proud that Sydney Parade Station had a fireplace in each of the two waiting rooms. He did mention, though, that he never saw a fire lit in them. Sandymount waiting rooms did not have fireplaces. Instead, as Mullee remembers, the first-class waiting room, as well as the ticket master's office, were heated by steam.

People who live not only on a road parallel to a railroad, but also near a level crossing, soon accept the noises of trains and bells as part of their normal background noise and become less aware of them. Any visitors staying with them might have a completely different perception of the acoustical surroundings, as the following story illustrates.

A man who did not live in Dublin had to go there for some weeks for business. For those weeks, he stayed with his sister and brother-in-law, who lived on a road parallel to the railway, not far from a station and a level crossing. This incident occurred during the time of steam locomotives and level crossings with gates. One morning, the visitor was late getting ready to leave the house for some reason. When he noticed the time, he clattered down the staircase and asked his hosts breathlessly, 'Has the 9.20 train gone yet?' His sister and her husband looked at him without understanding. How would they know? Trains came and went, but they hardly heard them at all and if so, they never connected the vague noise that might mean a train was passing with any special time.

It is not reported whether the visitor caught or missed the 9.20 train that day.

Further Reading

Bennett, Douglas. *Encyclopaedia of Dublin*. Dublin: Gill and Macmillan Ltd, 1991.

Davitt, Fr Tom. 'Getting hooked on trains: Sydney Parade 1934–1946', *IRRS Journal*, 187, 2015, pp. 277ff.

De Courcy, J.W. *The Liffey in Dublin*. Dublin: Gill & Macmillan Ltd, 1996.

Dixon Hardy, P. (publisher). *The Dublin and Kingstown Railway*. Dublin, 1834.

Ferris, Tom. *Irish Railways: A New History*. Dublin: Gill & Macmillan Ltd, 2009.

Goodbody, Rob. *The Metals: From Dalkey to Dún Laoghaire*. Dublin: Dún Laoghaire Rathdown County Council, 2010.

Horsfield, Brenda (ed.). *Steam Horse: Iron Road*. London: British Broadcasting Corporation (BBC), 1972.

Le Fanu, William Richard. *Seventy Years of Irish Life being Anecdotes and Reminiscences*. London: Edward Arnold, 1893.

Mullee, John Eugene. *Growing Up in Dublin: Reflections from the 1950s*. Houston, TX: Chac Mool Books, 2015.

Mulligan, Fergus. *One Hundred and Fifty Years of Irish Railway*. Belfast: The Appletree Press Ltd, 1983.

Murray, K.A. *Ireland's First Railway*. Dublin: Irish Railway Record Society, 1981.

Nolan, Kevin B. (ed.). *Travel and Transport in Ireland*. Dublin: Gill and Macmillan Ltd, 1973.

Ó Maitiú, Séamas. *Dublin's Suburban Towns 1834–1930*. Dublin: Four Courts Press Ltd, 2003.

Shedd, Thomas Clark. 'Railroads and Locomotives', in *The New Encyclopaedia Britannica in 30 Volumes*, Macropaedia Volume 15, 15th edition. Chicago, 1980, pp. 477–95

Thackeray, William Makepeace. *The Irish Sketch Book and Critical Reviews.* London: Smith, Elder & Co., 1879.

Walsh, Pat. *Images of Ireland: Dún Laoghaire-Rathdown.* Dublin: Nonsuch Publishing, 2005.

Whittock, N. *A Picturesque Guide through Dublin.* London, Dublin and Liverpool, 1846

Picture Credits

All images are the author's own unless listed: Page 11 Georgius Agricola, *De re Metallica* (Basel: Froben 1556), p 343 (page number refers to the translation into English by Herbert Clark Hoover and Lou Henry Hoover, published by Dover Publications Inc., New York, 1950); Page 12 Georgius Agricola: *De re Metallica* (Basel: Froben 1556) p 156 (page number refers to the translation into English by Herbert Clark Hoover and Lou Henry Hoover, published by Dover Publications Inc., New York, 1950); Page 25 Map of the route of the Dublin & Kingstown Railway. Drawn and engraved by B.R. Davies for the Society for the Diffusion of Useful Knowledge (SDUK), 1837; Page 30 Copyright https://commons.wikimedia.org/wiki/File:Charles_Blacker_Vignoles.jpg; Page 31 https://commons.wikimedia.org/wiki/File:William_Dargan_-_Project_Gutenberg_eText_17293.jpg; Page 32 Letters from Professor Thomas J. Mulvany R.H.A. to his eldest son William T. Mulvany Esq. Royal Commissioner of Public Works Ireland, picture after p. 34 https://ia600209.us.archive.org/9/items/cu31924008646105/cu31924008646105.pdf; Page 33 Journal of the Cork Historical and Archaeological Society, 1915, Vol. 21, No.108 pages 180–6 http://www.thosebefore.com/g14/p14444.htm; Page 35 Second report on Public Works in Ireland, 1834, No. 18, Plan 6; Page 36 Taken from a postcard; Page 37 Top of page: Taken from an postcard; Page 37 Bottom of page: Manning Robertson, *Dún Laoghaire: The History, Scenery and Development of the District*. Dún Laoghaire Borough Corporation, 1936, p. 23; Page 45 'Thirteen Views on The Dublin and Kingstown Railway', P. Dixon Hardy, Dublin, 1834; Page 46 P. Dixon Hardy (ed.), *Dublin Penny Journal*, Vol. 3, No. 125, p. 165; Page 47 Dublin & Kingstown Railway Second-Class Carriage, E. Heyden, *Dublin Penny Journal* 26 December 1835; Page 48 Illustration from the first Brockhaus edition, 1837; Page 50 Taken from a postcard; Page 54 © Dawgz, English Wikipedia; Page 54 Wills Cigarette Cards, Railway Engines 1936; Page 55 © Albert Bridge, reproduced under

About the Author

Kurt Kullmann was born and grew up in the Rhineland in Germany. He studied in Würzburg and Bonn, graduating with an MSc in Mineralogy. Later, he received the German equivalent of the Higher Diploma in Education and worked for twenty-five years as teacher. During this time, he graduated from Cologne University with a PhD.

Dr Kurt Kullmann.

He is married to Catherine Donovan Kullmann from Sandymount and they have three sons. In 1999, they moved back into the house in which Catherine grew up. After they had retired, they both started to write. Catherine writes historical novels and Kurt writes books about local history. Kurt now has German and Irish citizenship. He is a founding member of the Ballsbridge, Donnybrook and Sandymount Historical Society, as well as a member of the Old Dublin Society and the Förderkreis Historisches Walberberg. His earlier books *Rugby Town. The sporting history of D4*, *The Little Book of Sandymount* and *Four Sisters. The History of Ringsend, Irishtown, Sandymount and Merrion* have also been published by The History Press.

Notes

1   *The New Encyclopaedia Britannica in 30 Volumes*, Micropaedia Volume 15, 15th edition, Chicago, 1980, p. 540.

2   Thomas Clark Shedd, 'Railroads and Locomotives', in *The New Encyclopaedia Britannica in 30 Volumes*, Macropaedia Volume 15, 15th edition, Chicago, 1980, p. 477.

3   John E. Mullee, *Growing up in Dublin: Reflections from the 1950s*. Houston, TX: Chac Mool Books, 2015, p. 206. Quoted with the permission of John E. Mullee.

4   http://www.dun-laoghaire.com/harbour.html (accessed May 2017).

5   'Reports of the Commissioners appointed to consider and recommend a General System of Railways for Ireland. Presented to both Houses of Parliament by command of Her Majesty. 1838', in John Gibson Lockhart (ed.), *The Quarterly Review*, Vol. LXIII, 1839, p. 14f.

6   'Reports of the Commissioners appointed to consider and recommend a General System of Railways for Ireland. Presented to both Houses of Parliament by command of Her Majesty. 1838', in John Gibson Lockhart (ed.), *The Quarterly Review*, Vol. LXIII, 1839, p. 16f.

7   Thomas Drummond, Sir John Burgoyne, Prof. Peter Barlow, Richard J. Griffith, *Second and final report of the Royal Commission appointed to inquire into the Manner in which Railway Communications can be Most Advantageously Promoted in Ireland*, 13 June 1838, p. 89.

8   K.A. Murray, *Ireland's First Railway*. Dublin: Irish Railway Record Society, 1981, chapters 1 and 2.

9   Peter O'Keeffe & Tom Simmington, *Irish Stone Bridges: History and Heritage*. Revised by Rob Goodbody. Newbridge: Irish Academic Press, 2016, p. 349.

10 *The Post Office Annual Directory for 1845, Dublin, Printed for the Letter Carriers of the General Post Office 1845.* Annex after p. 676.

11 William Makepeace Thackeray, *The Irish Sketch Book and Critical Reviews.* London: Smith, Elder & Co., 1879, p. 7.

12 'Reports of the Commissioners appointed to consider and recommend a General System of Railways for Ireland. Presented to both Houses of Parliament by command of Her Majesty. 1838', in John Gibson Lockhart (ed.), *The Quarterly Review,* Vol. LXIII, 1839, p. 38.

13 N. Whittock, *A Picturesque Guide through Dublin,* London, Dublin and Liverpool 1846, p. 27.

14 http://www.turtlebunbury.com/published/published_books/ docklands/westland_row/pub_books_docklands_wr_pearsestation. html (accessed January 2017, the printed book does not give the measurements).

15 Thomas Drummond, Sir John Burgoyne, Prof. Peter Barlow, Richard J. Griffith, *Second and final report of the Royal Commission appointed to inquire into the Manner in which Railway Communications can be Most Advantageously Promoted in Ireland,* 13 June 1838, p. 103.

16 Stephen Johnson, *Johnson's atlas and gazetteer of the railways in Ireland.* Leicester: Midland Publishing, 1997, p. 84, as quoted in Séamas Ó Maitiú, *Dublin's Suburban Towns 1834–1930,* p. 147.

17 *Bradshaw's Descriptive Railway Hand-Book of Great Britain and Ireland,* 1863, Section II, p. 82.

18 K. A. Murray, *Ireland's First Railway.* Dublin: Irish Railway Record Society, 1981, p. 89.

19 K. A. Murray, *Ireland's First Railway.* Dublin: Irish Railway Record Society, 1981, p. 88.

20 K. A. Murray, *Ireland's First Railway.* Dublin: Irish Railway Record Society, 1981, p. 200.

21 Brenda Horsfield (ed.), *Steam Horse: Iron Road.* London: British Broadcasting Corporation (BBC), 1972, p. 77.

22 Bilder-Conversations-Lexikon für das deutsche Volk. Ein Handbuch zur Verbreitung gemeinnütziger Kenntnisse und zur Unterhaltung. In vier Bänden. Erster Band A–E. Mit 320 Abbildungen und 17 Landkarten. Leipzig: F.A. Brockhaus, 1837, p. 643.

23 W. R. Le Fanu, *Seventy Years of Irish Life being Anecdotes and Reminiscences.* London: Edward Arnold, 1893, p. 203.

24 K.A. Murray, *Ireland's First Railway*. Dublin: Irish Railway Record Society, 1981, p. 76.

25 http://en.wikipedia.org/wiki/Dublin_Area_Rapid_Transit#History (accessed January 2017).

26 http://en.wikipedia.org/wiki/Downpatrick_and_County_Down_Railway (accessed May 2017).

27 K.A. Murray, *Ireland's First Railway*. Dublin: Irish Railway Record Society, 1981, p. 94ff.

28 Quoted in K.A. Murray, *Ireland's First Railway*. Dublin: Irish Railway Record Society, 1981, p. 227.

29 K.A. Murray, *Ireland's First Railway*. Dublin: Irish Railway Record Society, 1981, p. 225.

30 Peter Costello, *Dublin Churches*. Dublin: Gill and Macmillan Ltd, 1989, p. 34.

31 John E. Mullee, *Growing up in Dublin: Reflections from the 1950s*. Houston, TX: Chac Mool Books, 2015, p. 241. Quoted with the permission of John E. Mullee.

32 *The Irish Times*, Wednesday, 19 July 2017, Commercial Property section, p. 8.

33 *The Dublin Penny Journal*, No. 103, Vol. II, 1834, p. 404f.

34 K.A. Murray, *Ireland's First Railway*. Dublin: Irish Railway Record Society, 1981, p. 177.

35 John E. Mullee, *Growing up in Dublin: Reflections from the 1950s*. Houston, TX: Chac Mool Books, 2015, p. 218. Quoted with the permission of John E. Mullee.

36 http://blackrock.ie/history-of-blackrock/ (accessed April 2017).

37 http://www.dia.ie/architects/view/3632/MULVANY,+JOHN+SKIPTON#tab_works (accessed March 2017).

38 *The Dublin Penny Journal*, No. 103, Vol. II, 1834, p. 404f.

39 K.A. Murray, *Ireland's First Railway*. Dublin: Irish Railway Record Society, 1981, p. 116.

40 http://www.dia.ie/architects/view/3632/MULVANY,+JOHN+SKIPTON#tab_works (accessed March 2017).

41   For details, contact Dún Laoghaire-Rathdown County Council.

42 http://www.dia.ie/architects/view/3632/MULVANY,+JOHN+SKIPTON#tab_works (accessed May 2017).

43   http://www.dun–laoghaire.com/harbour.html (accessed May 2017).

44   Fr Tom Davitt, CM, 'Getting hooked on trains: Sydney Parade 1934–
     1946', *IRRS Journal*, 187, 2015, pp. 277ff.

45   John E. Mullee, *Growing up in Dublin. Reflections from the 1950s.*
     Houston, TX: Chac Mool Books, 2015, p. 206f. Quoted with the
     permission of John E. Mullee.

46   John E. Mullee, *Growing up in Dublin. Reflections from the 1950s.*
     Houston, TX: Chac Mool Books, 2015, p. 211f. Quoted with the
     permission of John E. Mullee.

The destination for history
www.thehistorypress.co.uk